ISBN 978-1-330-72486-6
PIBN 10097323

1 MONTH OF
FREE
READING

at

www.ForgottenBooks.com

By purchasing this book you are eligible for one month membership to ForgottenBooks.com, giving you unlimited access to our entire collection of over 700,000 titles via our web site and mobile apps.

To claim your free month visit:

www.forgottenbooks.com/free97323

WILLIAM JAMES AND HENRI BERGSON

A STUDY IN CONTRASTING THEORIES OF LIFE

By

HORACE MEYER KALLEN, PH.D.
of the University of Wisconsin

THE UNIVERSITY OF CHICAGO PRESS
CHICAGO, ILLINOIS

Composed and Printed By
The University of Chicago Press
Chicago, Illinois, U.S.A.

TO

WILLIAM JAMES

My Master

PREFACE

In the spring of 1912 I was asked to give a series of talks on the relation between the philosophies of William James and *H*enri Bergson. This book is the outcome of the meditations which compliance with that request demanded. I have sought in it to draw the "counterfeit presentment of two brothers," brothers in that they are the children of the same age, that the same blood of its characteristic and perhaps unique tradition runs in the veins of their thought, and also, it may be, in that their individualities are so strikingly distinct and unique.

"There is," William James writes somewhere, "very little difference between one man and another; but what little there is, is very important." The difference between James and Bergson has seemed to me much more than little, and of an importance difficult to calculate in advance; for the difference turns on what is ultimately a philosophic prevision of the future and a philosophic summation of the past.

James's theory of life seems to me to face forward, to be an expression of the age's underlying and hence vaguely felt and unformulated tendencies. Bergson's theory of life sums itself up as a consummation of the philosophic tradition, restated in the modes of thought and harmonized with the modes of feeling of the age.

For this reason it has been easier to portray Bergson's philosophy than James's. Bergson has a system in which there is logical relation between premise and conclusion, a relation so complete and integrative, indeed, that it is difficult to state any single opinion of Bergson's plausibly without becoming involved at once in a restatement of the whole system. His doctrines literally "interpenetrate," and have thus made necessary a certain amount of repetition in the exposition of them. To portray James's philosophy, on the contrary, has required much direct quotation, partly because of the novelty of his opinions, partly because of the existence of some difference among philosophers concerning just what was central and important in James's own mind. James, more than any other protagonist in the history of thought, was free from that "certain blindness in human beings." His mind and eye were alert to the unique, the individual, hence the *important*, in all phases of life and reflection (it is said of him that he used to put an opponent's case better than his own); he could so think himself into a cause as to become, for the moment, dramatically identical with it, to the exclusion of everything else. His sympathetic and persuasive statement of one phase of the Bergsonian point of view, for example, has led many careless readers to regard him as a Bergsonian; and of the position of the "psychical researchers," as a spiritist, and so on; while his readiness to entertain and to try out any philosophical hypothesis has led various readers to consider him irrevocably committed to this or that philosophic dogma. His attitude toward "panpsychism" (see the concluding passages in *Some Problems of Philosophy*) is an example.

Now readers approaching so myriad-minded and empirical a thinker as James will, if they are philosophical, approach him with preconceptions, and if they are friendly, they will attribute their preconceptions to him. The portraits they draw of him will consequently be far more expressive of their own views than of James's. If I seem to claim for the present portrait a greater authenticity, it is only because I acquired my own theory of life at his feet, and because in five years of close and intimate personal contact with him I attained to a definite perception of what he regarded as central and what tangential in his *Weltanschauung*.

Of the six chapters of the book, two, in slightly different form, have been printed before, the first in the *Philosophical Review*, the fourth in *Mind*, and I acknowledge with thanks the editors' permissions to reprint these chapters. To my friends *Dr*. H. M. Sheffer, Mr. Alfred *D*. Sheffield, and *Dr*. *H*. G. Brown I owe a greater debt than I can repay for careful examination of the proofs and many valuable suggestions.

HORACE M. KALLEN

BOSTON, MASSACHUSETTS
August 24, 1914

CONTENTS

xi

CHAPTER I

RADICAL EMPIRICISM AND THE PHILO-SOPHIC TRADITION

The vision of the philosopher and the perception of the artist have this in common: they both ingest an existence alien in its nature and interests to the human mind, and they both re-create it, giving it color and form which the soul desires but does not find, character and effects which the spirit yearns for but cannot discover. The marbles of *P*hidias and the philosophy of *P*lato, the canvases of Raphael and the conceptions of *D*escartes, the poems of Goethe and the dialectic of *H*egel, all obey the same impulse and express the same will—an impulse to make over unsuitable realities into satisfactory ideas, a will to remodel discordant nature into happy civilization. Indeed, all cultures own this parentage, and rest, together with philosophy and art, the inevitable offspring of the creative imagination. Experience as it comes, comes full of shocks and checks:

it obstructs the will, it deceives the mind, it disrupts into tumult the even, onward flow of life. The will seeks the good and finds evil; the mind desires order and encounters disorder; life seeks to expand into the harmonies of its kind and finds itself constricted, repressed, and even self-opposed. Plural, chaotic, always full of a potential menace, experience, coming so, is not to be endured. The mind must of its own motion make it over, and its re-creations are the arts and philosophy. A painted fire pleases without burning, a sculptured hero has power to delight without power to destroy. But the creations of the artist are at once less radical and more enduring than the creations of the philosopher. The artist works upon the solid stuff of experience itself, eliminating, adding, molding, until this stuff bears the shape of his heart's desire. The philosopher, however, tends to spurn altogether the stuff of experience and to carve a world of his desire alone. Is felt reality manifold, embattled, chaotic? The philosopher casts it aside; as such, it is mere appearance: true reality is one, harmonious, orderly. Is felt reality alien in substance, oppugnant to man in its nature and effects? So, it is to be set aside as mere appearance: its real nature is spiritual, its true face is the face of God. Do the actualities of experience show human life ever-ending in its period, never continued? Then these actualities are false actualities, pure deception: in fact and in truth each man's life goes on unceasingly. Does the world offer hindrances in all directions to life's free flow, frustrating its desires, betraying its interests, binding its every movement with a chain of causes? This behavior of the world must be set aside as mere appearance: in reality man is in no sense bond, his desires are already attained, his interests accomplished, his spontaneity assured. In brief, the universe, like a Japanese mummer, wears a hideous mask of multiplicity, materiality, necessity, and death, behind which whoever will look may behold the joyous features of its unity and spirituality, its assurance of human immortality and human freedom. These are the traits of the real; all else is mere appearance.

And so, from Thales to Royce, philosophy has concerned itself with seeking proof, almost unexceptionally, for one or all of these four desiderates—the unity of the world; the existence of God, in some form of spiritistic substance, from theism to pantheism; the immortality of the soul; the freedom of the will. At the very least, the unity of the world was asserted. Even materialisms and atheisms refused to concede that to the actualities of experience. And as the full quota of these excellences, said to lie beneath and to support the flux, cannot without logical contradiction all be defended at once, most systems of philosophy are content with defending two, or at most three, of them. Thus the unity of the world is incompatible with the freedom of the will, the freedom of the will with the existence of an omnipotent, omniscient, and well-disposed God. Individual immortality is oppugnant to cosmic unity, and cosmic unity to theistic divinity. These oppugnances, coupled with the mind's natural demand for logical consistency, have given rise to the typical philosophic "problems," and in the shuffle of adjudicating the rights of the "problems" by dialectic the data of immediate experience have been completely neglected. When these did get any consideration whatever, beyond such consideration as is implied in neglect, they were at once transmuted by means of "forms of the understanding" or of "unknowables" into the substance of some desiderate; and when it was acknowledged, as by Kant, that the data of immediate experience could not in these forms yield any proof of the sublime desiderates, they were segregated from experience, and the desiderates were enacted into postulates of conduct. This compromise, which was rather a refusal to face the metaphysical dilemma than a resolution thereof, could not endure. Kant's chief contribution to the history of philosophy is the dialectic triad of the transcendental method. Transcendentalism itself goes, however, the way of traditional metaphysics, substituting in the ancient way desiderates for data, ideals for facts. It is, in a word, no less than the older metaphysic, essentially the vicarious fulfilment of unsatisfied desire, a compensation in discourse for a disappointment in reality.

The metaphysical tradition is not, however, the only tradition designated by the term "philosophy." This term once meant the total field of thinking about experience. As, in the course of time, various special ranges of thought became enriched with collections of accurately observed data, yielding a common formula descriptive of their behavior, these dropped off and became special sciences. Mathematics was probably first, then astronomy, then physics, and in the three hundred years' duration of modern positive science all the special sciences whose names are now so familiar. One range of investigation seems none the less indissolubly linked to philosophy: this range is the human mind, for it is the mind's ultimate aims and inward character that philosophy seeks to make reality conform to. Now those philosophers who are known as the English empiricists devoted themselves almost exclusively to a study of the human mind, its content, its behavior, its laws. They are known, significantly, as philosophers, not as psychologists, and though psychology makes today pretensions to being a positive science, it is not less closely allied to philosophy than in the days of Locke and *H*artley and *H*ume. The empirical bias of these Englishmen gave them this superiority over the traditional metaphysicians: they tended to face mental facts as facts, not in the light of compensatory desiderates. The "problem" concerning these latter did indeed, as Locke tells us, give rise to his investigations, and it is true that Berkeley made a metaphysical special plea by means of his researches. But in the long run they did face the facts, and the outcome of the tradition in *H*ume's famous conclusions was nearer envisaging the actual processes of experience than anything prior or contemporary.

Nearer, I say. But nearer only when the experiential flux itself or the human mind taken in isolation is not too closely scrutinized. With respect to both of these, important or essential data were missed or translated, not permitted to speak for themselves. *Principles, relations,* connections, denied to reality, were unwittingly set in the mind, and the opposition between the mind and reality was made such that the former's integral place in the latter was ignored. Take the case of "necessary connexion." This *H*ume reduced to a psychological habit of expectation, setting this relation altogether in the mind. But in so doing he failed to observe that acquiring a habit demands just that kind of modifiability designated by "necessary connexion," and that hence, in crediting the mind with an *acquired* habit, he credited the universe in so far forth with an actually experienced "necessary connexion." The fact is that the same desideration which claims for unity in the world a reality superior to diversity claims for unity in discourse a truth superior to diversity. *H*ume was as much a rationalist in his procedure as he was an empiricist in his conclusions. The logical implications of premise and consequence were in fact of greater importance to him than the actual oppugnances and counter-implications of experience. He aimed, not to be correct, but to be consistent. And in his attempt to be consistent, i.e., to move only within the range of chosen premises to their logical conclusions, he missed envisaging reality as it is and substituted therefor a picture-reality *logically deduced.*

Now such a picture, like an artist's drawing, will have that unity and consistency and satisfactoriness which the mind desiderates from all things. But these are always attained at the cost of eliminating "irrelevancies," solving "contradictions," dressing up facts, whether or no. And all the while, just these "irrelevancies," just these "contradictions," just these bare facts have in and of themselves the same right and status in reality as the data saved and transformed. The first to recognize and acknowledge this right was William James.[1] Where, throughout the nineteenth century, philosophers persisted either in discriminating between appearance and reality in such wise as to formulate reality in one or all of the

[1] Cf. "On Some Omissions of Introspective Pyschology," *Mind*, IX (1884), 1–26; *The Will to Believe*, p. 299: "What Psychical Research Has Accomplished."

compensatory terms of God, freedom, immortality, and cosmic unity; or where, in response to the pressure of rapidly growing sciences, men faced fact, only to change it in such wise as thereby to satisfy the inner need for "logical consistency," James insisted that each event of experience must be acknowledged for what it appears to be, and heard for its own claims. To neither doubt nor belief, datum nor preference, term nor relation, value nor fact, did he concede superiority over the others. Each had for him the same metaphysical claim, the same right to opportunity to make that claim good. Hence he pointed out to the rationalist the co-ordinate presence in experience of so much more than reason; he called the monist's attention to the world's diversity; the pluralist's to its unity. He said to the materialist: You shall not shut your eyes to the immaterial; to the spiritualist: You shall take cognizance also of the non-spiritual. He was a rationalist without unreason, an empiricist without prejudice. His empiricism was *radical,* preferring correctness to consistency, truth to logic. All things, he urged, however and whenever they occur in experience, must be taken at their face value, for what they are as they occur, and they must not be mistrusted until they have proved themselves untrustworthy. *Pure experience knows no favorites.* It admits into reality, without making over, evil as well as good, discontinuities as well as continuities, unhuman as well as human, plurality as well as unity, chance and novelty as well as order and law. It is a record and a description, not a transmutation; an expression, not a compensation. As a philosophy its principle is that of direct democracy, and William James, who first gave it voice, is the first democrat in metaphysics.

Now democratic metaphysics does not readily submit to systematization. A philosophic system is essentially a work of art. Like a picture or a drama or a symphony, it is the cunning arrangement of certain selected premises and their explication, according to dialectic law. It invariably omits more than it envisages, alters and harmonizes all that it touches, concerns itself, in a word, with consistency rather than with truth. There is no philosophic turpitude in errors of fact; the metaphysician's unpardonable sin lies in error of form, in self-contradiction. His reputation, like the painter's, tends to depend far more on his technique than on his subject-matter. The universe, however, exceeds technique. A systematic treatment of it harmonious with correctness is out of question. On every side appear "inconsistencies" and "irrelevancies" demanding equal treatment with the favored instances, claiming to be, no less than those, essentials. Each datum, moreover, offers its own seductive implications; each crosses, penetrates into, and interferes with, others. Reality comes, from moment to moment, as an infinite mélange of systems, never as system in itself. But reality, coming so, comes as every man must meet it in perception, when it compels his attention on peril of his life, challenging him to choose which of its protean faces he will, to engage and to conquer. Hence, what this challenge evokes from him actually cannot be a special envisagement of his perception's never-completed total, called philosophy. *He* is required to operate rather than to envisage, to save himself rather than to see. And he meets the requirement by a method of treating reality piecemeal, which under one set of circumstances is common-sense; under another, science; under another, religion; under another, art; under still another, philosophy. In each case one particular bit or combination of bits of reality is used as an instrument to render the residuum more congenial to mankind; each is a special sort of tool, serving a common end. And a system of philosophy is nothing more. It harnesses the universe in the lines of some preferred order, making it more akin to man and more amenable to his interests. No less so do common-sense, religion, art, and science. They all unify, assure, conserve. They are all tools and modes of life, and are all as such *pragmatic*.

If this be true, pragmatism is not merely a new name for old ways of thinking; it is a new name for *all* ways of thinking. In view of the general attitude of its opponents, of the elaborate instruments of argumentation set in motion against it, of the appearance of new overshadowing issues, this observation gets the twist of paradox, for in the light of it the opponents must have been stultifying merely themselves, not the pragmatists. Yet nothing could have been more natural than the controversy over pragmatism, and nothing more inevitable than the shift of ground to other issues.

To begin with, it is only through the explication of the pragmatic rule itself that thinkers became conscious of the motives which, in the spirit's deep, underlie the persistent construction of philosophies. In ancient times the Aristotelian wonder had been accepted as sufficient; and this wonder stirred no further wonder about its own nature and origin, the intimacy of the sentiment and its ultimacy being undistinguished. The mediaevals wished only to reconcile brute experience with the Christian theory of life, and held the purpose of philosophy to be the confirmation of theology. That theology itself is only philosophy of a particular flavor and color, they failed, on the whole, to observe. They held it simply and frankly for a method of confirming desiderates whose existence was an unquestioned dogma. The "critical philosophy" was the first explicitly to deny confirmatory powers to metaphysics and veridical assurance to theology, but it reserved the desiderates of both as the *sine qua non* of conduct, and demonstrated God and freedom and immortality by the needs of action, as it demonstrated unity by the "laws of thought." But these needs and these laws remained unquestioned dogmas, no less unwarranted by the processes of experience than the desiderates of the mediaevals. Schopenhauer sought to found philosophy on the "consciousness that the non-existence of the world is just as possible as its existence." This was going deep, but it was not going down to an inspection of this consciousness and the possibilities that it recognized. It remained for him an ultimate fact, whereas it is not ultimate at all, being no more than barest schematic formulation of the growing experiential flux, of becoming, where things truly are and are not at the same time, and hence compel the mind to special alertness. Schopenhauer was perhaps the last, till William James, to have been troubled about the origin of metaphysics. *P*hilosophers of our own age concerned themselves little about the spring and origin of their speculative activity. Their interest in philosophy was, on the whole, professional rather than human; for them thinking has turned into a self-sufficing exercise in dialectic, where it used to be an adaptation to a not over-kindly world. *P*hilosophy has fallen into the position of a toper whose first drink was taken to save his life and who ever afterward lived to drink. In a word, philosophy is gripped by the inveterate habit of hypostatizing the instrument.

*H*ypostasis of the instrument is not the peculiar vice of philosophy alone. When science sacrifices observed fact to hypothetic law, when art conserves a technique, such as impressionism, and foregoes beauty, when government puts the perfection of its machinery above the happiness of the people, when religion wars over doctrine and ritual and neglects salvation, there occurs hypostasis of the instrument. The reason is not far to seek. The world we live in is one in which we happened, not one which was made for us. If it had been made for us we should not live in it as we do. Existence would have been beatitude and thought divinity, self-absorbed and self-possessed. But we live only at the risk of life and only too often barter living for *a* living. In every region of experience, from ideals to things, there is a struggle to be, as utter and profound as it is implacable. In every region very few are the fit who survive. Not a moment's thought, not a pleasure felt, nor an idea realized, but keeps its head above the flux at the cost of innumerable suppressed and lost. What is man but a battle-field of interests, a field of a few dominant ones and a horde starving, unfulfilled? To possess little he must forego much, and what he lives by, what keeps him in so far forth, unsubmerged, becomes the more precious for what it has cost. It is the all-saving tool, won at great hazard, used with constant risk, and preserved with constant cost. A hypothesis, a religion, a form of government sweeps all appropriate data under its beneficent control, divests them of their power to harm, prepares them to feed the proper life of man. To conserve these, henceforward, becomes more important than the conservation of their end. For their end, although no less than they, fleeting and elusive, is still inalienable; in its manifold intimacy of feeling, life's goal is everywhere no more than life. But the instrument, fashioned always of some especial fragment selected from the experiential complex, is not so inalienable. Initially it is a nature foreign to man's, distrained from its own ways to life's uses, and at every moment it may slip from the hands and go those ways. *H*ence it becomes an ultimate concern. It signifies inward possession, where the goal signifies only desire; it is the key to the heaven where the treasure is laid up, while the goal is only the yearning for the treasure, an uneasiness and irritation until possessed. Inevitably, therefore, the instrument, being always the more immediate and certain possession, assumes a constantly greater importance, and ends like the Arab's camel, by crowding its master out of the tent. There arises a worship of the instrument. And about this worshipful object is it that men fight their greatest quarrels in science and religion and philosophy. What could have been more bitter than the quarrel between the theologians and Galileo, on the theologians' side? The fact announced by Galileo made a cherished instrument useless. Or the feeling among theologians themselves concerning such questions as: Shall the priest use three or two fingers in uttering the benediction? *D*oes the miracle of transubstantiation occur in the sacrament? Are indulgences valid? Is grace better had by partial or by total immersion? Is the pope infallible? These are matters, among numberless others, the Christian world has not ceased to quarrel about. They are notably merely *means;* the end, salvation, all Christians are agreed on. Or more largely: What was the issue in the wars of opposed faiths, as between Moslems and Christians? Not heaven, nor yet the nature of God. Concerning these there is no inconsiderable unanimity. The issue concerns the instruments whereby these are to be attained —Mohammed the prophet of Allah versus Jesus the only-begotten son of God. Or yet in art, do men quarrel about beauty or about technique? The impressionist against the realist, the futurist against the classicist, defend *means* of painting, making these the paramount issue, and forgetting the end in the means. There is no need to multiply examples: men tend to differ chiefly about instruments. They do not quarrel about the wine, they quarrel about the bottles.

*P*hilosophy is perhaps least of all exempt from this quarrel. The end which philosophers seek is the same. The empirical reality they seek it in is the same. The urgency that compels the search is the same. Schools and systems do not debate about starting-points and stopping-places. They debate about vehicles of transit. *D*o we secure ourselves in experience more effectively by thinking the world in terms of matter or in terms of spirit? *D*o we gain our ends better by thinking reality as altogether free or altogether bond? as one or many? a block or a sandheap? as divinely controlled or as mechanical? as ultimately good or ultimately bad? Each of these predicating words, if it means anything at all, means some specific datum of immediate experience, one of an infinite number of such in the warring flux. And according to the answer you choose to make to any of these questions you refashion this vast residuum in the image of this one and announce it to behave after the manner of this one. So, you unify all your world, are prepared for the chances and shocks of new experience, and go your way rejoicing. Your philosophy becomes your most precious possession, your device eternally and happily to rest in harmony with the residual universe; becomes, hence, the source and unshakable foundation of the reality of this end, and so itself alone, and not the residuum, the content and standard of creation. Instrument and end have changed places. No longer is it a question of the adequacy of the system to secure you in the world;

it is a question of the adequacy of the world to measure up to your standard system. If the world doesn't, so much the worse for the world. You then call it mere appearance. The true and abiding reality is your system.

Now, there are very many systems and each lays practically exclusive claim to the salvational power of metaphysical truth. Each refuses to be enumerated over a common denominator. But pragmatism, with its democratic presupposition in metaphysics, its perception that philosophy is fundamentally a method of using pieces of reality to control the remainder, but that it can never be a vision of the total, is just such an enumeration. For pragmatism all systems start on the same level; their opportunities are equal, and the superiority of one over another is eventual, not primary; to be achieved by works, not by an inborn and inoperative gift. To envisage philosophies thus is, however, to restore to perception the older relations of thoughts and things; it is to recall metaphysics to its original status and forgotten business. There was vexation in such a call, inevitably; and not a little of the controversy about pragmatism sprang from this unanalyzed vexation, sprang as a defense, against pragmatist challenge, of the hypostasis of the instrument which all compensational systems practice.[1]

But, furthermore, the exposition of pragmatism, the method and theory of truth, went on without much consideration of the undiscriminated immediacies of experience (the subject-matter of radical empiricism) to control which method was born. The exposition looked back, when it did look back, to science

[1] It is such hypostatizing treatment that gave rise to the much-debated analysis of pragmatism into thirteen mutually exclusive and contradictory varieties. But it is clear that there may easily be an infinite number of such, which, different, and even oppugnant with respect to each other, as hypostatized substances, will yet be unanimous and identical with respect to a common function. The lion and the lamb are intrinsically inimical, but under appropriate conditions functionally agreed to aim at the same thing, the conservation by each of his own life. Rivals for the hand of the same woman may seek to cut each other's throats, but they will both be agreed in glorifying the beloved. And so on. Only the hypostatization of function or the identification of function with structure or substance can cause and constitute the incompatibilities of which pragmatism is accused. And this accusation is only another example of the hypostatizing habit of philosophy.

only; but chiefly it looked forward, determining procedure in terms of "future consequences," desiderated and undesiderated. Now science itself is discriminative; and, though it rests more obviously than other human institutions on primary immediacies, the immediacies it *handles* are the primary ones already modified by such experience-stuffs as order and quantity. These pervasive contents of reality are highly excellent; they facilitate, as little else save "spirit" is supposed to do, the mind's prosperous movements among other realities. They become therefore easily the foremost subjects of hypostasis, which then seems to dominate their total range of influence. In scientific method, consequently, the opponents of pragmatism perceived what they thought was a morphological distinction between hypothesis and truth, but what actually is a functional one, truth being pragmatically no more than fit hypothesis. But this was enough to cause anti-pragmatists to attribute to the pragmatic exposition, not the character of a description of the genesis and

nature of method, but, by virtue of the psychologist's fallacy, the character belonging to
their own systems as *inoperative* instruments,
the character of one more hypostasis, additional
to those already existing. The unavoidable
stress on consequences, moreover, these being
the goals of desire (marked by "satisfaction"),
and thereby "terminal" to processes, served
to divert attention somewhat too much from
the situations out of which consequences grow,
with the result that the momentary structure
of method was substituted for its operative
movement, even by pragmatists themselves.
*P*ragmatism was then conceived, as by *P*apini,
after the analogy of a hotel corridor which
serves as a passageway for individual travelers
to their respective metaphysical rooms. But
in fact the metaphysical systems are not lodg-
ings: the lodging is the reality to which these
systems are applied. In fact, pragmatism is
not a passageway: it is a common *way of passing*, and each metaphysical system is a particu-
larization of this common way. What was
needful, therefore, for the right consideration

of pragmatism was the envisagement of the *terminus a quo* of method not less than the *terminus ad quem*, and particularly needful was the observation that method *is a way of passing* and not an architectonic of static intellectual faculties.   But the hypostatizing mind comes to rest in its hypostasis while the enduring world flows away beneath.   It is as unnatural for that mind to conceive its system as an instrument as it is for the healthy person who is not a student of physiology to be aware that he is breathing, or the ruminative cow that she thinks.   The discussion of method, hence, was never quite a discussion of method.   It edged always toward *prospective ultimacies* and finally got lost in these.   Interest turned to the logical as against the functional implications of method, and in consequence the field of analysis rapidly shifted.   Humanists got accused of absolute idealism, pluralists of monism, all pragmatists of self-contradiction;   there arose the formula of "absolute pragmatism," and so on, unendingly.   None the less, in all this time, as the field got more and more explored, the *terminus a quo* of method received a progressively greater emphasis and the *radical empiricism* and *tychism* from which, in fact, pragmatic method naturally flows became the dominant interest of pragmatic thinkers. Controversy about method melted thus into controversy about reality.

Radical empiricism aims, we have seen, to describe reality as it comes to cognition, to apprehend experience in its purity, before it has been worked on to satisfy our needs or remodeled to serve our interests. It refuses to act selectively, and by special emphasis on its selections to take the *logical* step which would drive it into a monism or an absolutism of any kind whatsoever. It lays no weightier emphasis on the mind than on nature, on environment than on organism, on concept than on percept. Being, for radical empiricism, is neutral, and demands chiefly a narrative of its behavior and a plan for meeting its events. These, radical empiricism points out, are the buds and bourgeons of a flux of a seething plurality of entities, each *there*, each trying to stay *with* if not *on*, and by the means of, its fellows. The "total," always exceeding itself from moment to moment, is not a whole, but an aggregate of *eaches*, each with a vote that it casts primarily for itself, each involving novelties, chances, mutations, and discretenesses as well as necessities and continuities and uniformities. These latter show themselves equally present in experience with the former, the former equally with the latter. Each *has* to be allowed for, whether or no. Thus, although recognizing human values, and indeed making them central, radical empiricism refuses to distort the world, as idealisms do, that these values may be eternally conserved; or to belittle value as such, as materialisms do, that the preferred excellence of a type of order may seem omnipotent. It acknowledges, for all things equally with spirit, the right and the will and the struggle to be. It accepts on the same level with human aspiration all its conditions and incumbrances, extenuating nothing, mitigating nothing, rejecting nothing, excusing nothing. Where it enforces, it enforces against inadequate emphasis, as in the case of "the will to believe"; where it defends, it defends against overemphasis and excess, as in its treatment of dogmatic naturalism. It seeks everywhere to avoid bias, and it is possible only when philosophy has ceased to be compensatory and has become expressive.

But systems are, as we have seen, the outcome of bias, of a passion for logical unity, on the one side, and for the conservation of valuable forms of existence, on the other. *H*ence radical empiricism is metaphysics which is expressible in an *attitude*, not in a system. It envisages the neutral starting-point from which all systems diverge and the common center into which, if alive and active, they converge. It is prior to systems just as life is prior to discourse, and it absorbs and supervenes on them in the same way. What radical empiricism can endow systematic philosophy with, hence, is first of all freedom of direction, flexibility in observation and procedure, and, secondly, fresh and distinctive premises for dialectic construction. It keeps throwing ever-new data into the focus of philosophic attention, emphasizing against the compensatory prejudice innumerable neglected contents of experience. Such are, for example, the observation of the democratic consubstantiality of every entity in experience with every other, of the existence of external relations, of the fluid and temporal nature of being. Start with any one of these as a premise, develop it with logical or sentimental consistency, and you get genuinely fresh and novel systematic philosophies. The newer developments of metaphysics in the temporalism of Bergson and the staticism of the new realists are such logical or sentimental explications.

Picture, if you will, the encounter with the mighty ancients of some young, mid-Victorian doctor of philosophy, dead before his time and entered by mischance into Elysium instead of heaven. Stumbling, diffident, and slow, he moves among the shadowy cypresses and laurels, over the floor of asphodel, all of a yearning over strange shapes beautiful, and half afraid, so gray the sourceless iridescent light, so fleet the shapes, the sounds so fugitive. But soon, through the dim alleys, he beholds a brightness, fading toward him in decrescent slopings. Toward that he turns, as moth to flame, first hovering, uncertain, then with straight, swift rush. Not here, however, can fall the mothen fate, to drop swiftly with scorched wings. This light and glow cannot destroy: they revive and strengthen, making the spirit whole. They that live in it arise from their pleasant seats to bid him welcome—Socrates and all the host that followed after, *P*lato and Aristotle, Euclides, Judaean *Phi*lo, even *P*lotinos—breaking a discourse of God, and the good, and man's soul everlasting. When he is refreshed they ask him, rare wanderer to Elysium since Christ brought forth his heaven, for news of the folk on earth.

He considers. What is there, among the brave translunary things that men discourse upon and hunger for, unknown to these, Aristotelians all, from *P*lato to this latest day? The living streams of thought live still with their life and shine with their colors. Shall he mention the new scholastics and their straining Godward? the life of them is Aristotle, and his alone their force. Or the idealists, for whom God is everywhere, his essence visible to men in ecstatic vision? What holds that essence that Plotinos saw not, that *P*armenides had not urged? And have not Epicureans and Stoics foreclosed all materialisms, and Skeptics and Academicians all criticisms? Contemporary philosophy, in so far as it embodies an actual and continuous tradition, contains nothing these Greeks had not presaged and foreshadowed—the persistent monism, the spiritualism, the devotion to eternity, to life, to the good.

The new immortal, then, would be hard put to it to find for the ancient thinkers philosophic news. For that he would have needed to postpone his advent into Elysium until the first decade of the twentieth century. *H*e would have needed to mark the enormous growth of positive science, the development of ethics and social theory as a part of biology, the application of biological conceptions to the study of mind—in a word, the tremendously fructifying effect of the *D*arwinian hypothesis applied to all possible fields of investigation and endeavor. Then he would have needed to note the extension of the field of application of this hypothesis until it became metaphysical, the consequent rise of radical empiricism and pragmatism, and the swift growth of philosophy in a genuinely fresh direction thereafter. This would have been genuine news to the ancients, of a philosophy having no semblance or echo of anything they knew, neither even in *Hera-cleitos* nor *Protagoras*. For the rectilinear, indeterminate flow of existence envisaged in radical empiricism is altogether different from the Logos-dominated merging of everything into its opposite in the *circular* movement of existence from fire to fire that Heracleitos thought to explain existence by. And the reputed formula of *Protagoras* is closer to subjectivism than to radical empiricism, for which existences must be given before they are judged. Man, thence, can be the measure only of the values and uses of things, not of their being. Only for the idealist is he the measure of their being, and with the idealists, until we have more data, *Protagoras* must be counted. The "new philosophy" is really new.

But the "new philosophy" is not radical empiricism alone, nor yet pragmatism. These terms designate what was to be the matrix and coincident part of a much varying tendency, which ramified particularly into two specific systems, each a type of metaphysical construction turning about distinctly novel data first thrown into relief by the investigations of William James.

These philosophies are the "new realism" of Edwin *H*olt and others, and the "temporalism" or vitalism of Bergson. Both may be treated as systematic elaborations of one or more elements of experience that radical empiricism has thrown into the center of attention. Thus the "new realism" tends to be democratic and pluralistic. It acknowledges the consubstantiality of every item of experience save "internal relations" and "pure duration." *H*aving found that the recognition of the externality of some relations is an effective instrument in solving one or more vexatious metaphysical problems—such as that of the relation of the mind to its object—it forthwith hypostatizes the instrument and petrifies it into a universal dogma, and recuts all relations in accord with the pattern it so creates. The world it desiderates, consequently, is empirical and particularistic, but also inert and powerless. Change and motion and continuity—when they are not insinuated through the back-door by being equated with relations—have to be attenuated to the condition of mere appearance, and cause must be frozen into a merely external relation holding forever between an antecedent and a consequent, i.e., into an ineffectuality. Still further, the sole type of order in such a world is the order of the "identity-logic," the order of human reason. The world possesses, hence, for the "new realism" an architectonic unity, analogous to the unity of *Plato's* system of ideas, with the profound difference that this unity is assumed to be the actual content of experience, and not its archetype; that it is generated empirically and positivistically in the manner of Comte, and not teleologically as a form of self-reproduction of the good, which is the manner of *Plato.* The "new realism" is new because it is radical empiricism. It is allied to the philosophic tradition because it gives that empiricism a compensatory significance by means of the "speculative dogma" concerning the externality of relations and of the intimacy and warmth of formal logic taken as universally regulative.

It has thus made hypostasis of two instruments, and by using formal logic and external relations as the measure of existence secures an unchallenged place among protagonists of the compensatory tradition.

To formulate the bearing of Bergson's temporalism on the empiricism of James is far more difficult. The influence of the "new realism" is yet to come; that of Bergson is at its height. Where the "new realism" is exceedingly recent, with very few pronouncements, all subsequent to the exposition of radical empiricism, the philosophy of Bergson has been receiving constant and systematic explication for more than a score of years. The similarities and differences between the new realism and radical empiricism are distinct and stand sharply defined: those between the latter and Bergsonian temporalism seem vague and confused and stand in need of explication. James and Bergson both perceive reality as flux; but are they in agreement concerning the detail of its movement and operation? They both entertain an "instrumental theory of knowledge";

they are both anti-intellectualistic and committed to evolutionism; but are these agreements more than agreements in tendency, in general directions of thought, or genuine agreement in concrete detail, perception for perception and opinion for opinion? Is James a Bergsonian and Bergson a Jamesian in method, in epistemology, in metaphysics? Is there unanimity on those ultimate topics of the nature of truth, the one and the many, freedom and chance, the character of mind and of matter and the relation between them, the nature and existence of God, the origin and destiny of man?

What, in a word, is the metaphysical insight and theory of life of each of these thinkers, and what is the relation of one to the other? Of priority there can be no question.[1] The series of investigations which culminated in the great *Principles of Psychology* were registered between 1874 and 1890 in various articles and reviews published in periodicals

[1] Cf. G. T. Sandeau, "Nouvelles modes en philosophie," *Journal des débats* (February 16, 1907); A. Chaumieux, "William James," *Revue des deux mondes* (October 15, 1910).

American and foreign. In the years 1884 appeared in *Mind*[1] the two articles embodying those doctrines which are most distinctive of James's psychological teaching and metaphysical outlook—the conception of thought as a stream, in which relations are as immediate data of perception as terms, and the conception of emotion as organic sensation. In his first book, published in 1889, M. Bergson cites the latter article.[2] Of the former, entitled "Some Omissions of Introspective *Psychology*," on the other hand, he categorically denies having had any knowledge.[3] Until the publication of *Matière et mémoire*, it would seem, the two thinkers developed their philosophies independently, and their unanimity, in so far as they are unanimous, is perhaps better to be attributed to the data they studied than to reciprocal influencing. But James's discovery of these data indisputably antedated Bergson's by some years.

[1] IX, 1–26, 188–205.   [2] *Time and Freewill*, p. 29.

[3] *Revue philosophique*, LX, 229, note.

Are they, however, the *same* data? To a considerable extent, undeniably so. Nor is there anything in the utterances of James concerning Bergson's vision to indicate that he was unaware of the exact limits of this identity. These are designated first of all by the coincidence of general direction—the temporalism, the instrumentalism, and the anti-intellectualism. In the second place, they include substantial agreement concerning the *function* of concepts. And finally they define the great pragmatist's acknowledgment of Bergson's service in providing him with cogent and acceptable grounds for entertaining a view he had long felt himself driven toward but could not "logically" accept. This view relates to the "compounding of consciousness." In his *A Pluralistic Universe*, William James had insisted that

the higher thoughts . . . . are psychic units, not compounds; but for all that, they may know together as a collective multitude the very same objects which under other conditions are known separately by as many simple thoughts.[1]

---

[1] *A Pluralistic Universe*, chap. v, 189.

In a note, he adds:

I hold to it still as the best description of an enormous number of our higher fields of consciousness. They demonstrably do not *contain* the lower states that know the same objects. Of other fields, however, this is not so true; so in the *Psychological Review* for 1895, Vol. II, p. 105 (see especially pp. 119–20), I frankly withdrew, in principle, my former objection to talking of fields of consciousness being made of simpler "parts," leaving the facts to decide the question in each special case.[1]

The facts, then, were the driving force against logical bias.

I found myself compelled to *give up logic*, fairly, squarely, irrevocably. It has an imperishable use in human life, but that use is not to make us theoretically acquainted with the essential nature of reality . . . . so I prefer bluntly to call reality if not irrational then at least non-rational in its constitution—and by reality here I mean reality where things *happen*, all temporal reality without exception. I find myself no good warrant for even suspecting the existence of any reality of a higher denomination than that distributed and strung along and flowing sort of reality we finite beings swim in. That is the sort of reality given us, and that is the sort with which logic is so incommensurable.[2]

[1] *Ibid.*, p. 338.

[2] *Ibid.*, pp. 212–13.

But:

I have now to confess . . . . that I should not now be emancipated, not now subordinate logic with so very light a heart, or throw it out of the deeper regions of philosophy to take its rightful and respectable place in the world of simple human practice, if I had not been influenced by a comparatively young and very original French writer, Professor Henri Bergson. *Reading his works is what has made me bold.* If I had not read Bergson, I should probably still be blackening endless pages of paper privately, in the hope of making ends meet that were never meant to meet, and trying to discover some mode of conceiving the behavior of reality which should leave no discrepancy between it and the accepted laws of the logic of identity. It is certain, at any rate, that without the confidence which being able to lean on Bergson's authority gives me I should never have ventured to *urge these particular views of mine* upon this ultra-critical audience.

I must, therefore, *in order to make my own views* more intelligible, give some preliminary account of the Bergsonian philosophy. But . . . . *I must confine myself only to the features that are essential to the present purpose,* and not entangle you with collateral details, however interesting otherwise. For our present purpose, then, *the essential contribution of Bergson to philosophy is his criticism of intellectualism.*[1]

The effect of Bergson, we may observe, was on the one hand to confirm William James in

---

[1] *Op. cit.*, pp. 214-15. The italics are mine.

his opinions concerning the *alogical* nature of reality and on the other to supply him with an authoritative criticism of intellectualism, to supplement his own, which, cogent enough to most of his friends and pupils, seemed to him insufficient. With respect to these general propositions, and to these only, may James be said to hold the Bergsonian philosophy, and with respect to these Bergson is as much a Jamesian as James a Bergsonian. These express a unanimity of tendency, not of concrete vision, and the discussion of Bergson in *A Pluralistic Universe* shows beyond the shadow of a doubt that James is concerned with Bergson only with respect to this tendency, going, *in re* of the particulars of insight, his own way.

I have to confess [he writes] that Bergson's originality is so profuse that many of his ideas baffle me entirely. I doubt whether any one understands him all over, so to speak; and I am sure that he would himself be the first to see that this must be, and to confess that things which he himself has not yet thought out clearly had yet to be mentioned and have a tentative place assigned them in his philosophy.[1]

[1] *Ibid.*, p. 226.

And throughout the chapter, wherever Bergson's critique of intellectualism implies more than a mere designation of the flowing reality which intellect fails to envisage, the description of that reality is James's, not Bergson's. Thus, James writes of time, for example:

> If a bottle had to be emptied by an infinite number of successive decrements, it is mathematically impossible that the emptying should ever terminate. In point of fact, however, bottles and coffee-pots empty themselves by a finite number of decrements, each of definite amount. Either a whole drop emerges or nothing emerges from the spout. If all change went thus drop-wise, so to speak, *if real time sprouted or grew by units of duration of determinate amount*, just as our perceptions of it grow by pulses, there would be no Zenonian paradoxes or Kantian antinomies to trouble us. . . . . Time itself comes in drops.[1]

If its analysis by the conceptualization of the identity logic leads to paradoxes, all thinkers save Bergson persist that the remedy for the failure of this logic is more of the same. Bergson "alone denies that mere conceptual logic can tell us what is impossible or possible in the world of being or fact":[2]

---

[1] *Op. cit.*, p. 231.　　[2] *Ibid.*, p. 243.

When we conceptualize, we cut out and fix, and exclude everything but what we have fixed. A concept means a *that-and-no-other*. Conceptually time excludes space; motion and rest exclude each other; approach excludes contact; presence excludes absence; unity excludes plurality; independence excludes relativity; "mine" excludes "yours"; this connexion excludes that connexion—and so on indefinitely; whereas in the real concrete sensible flux of life experiences compenetrate each other so that it is not easy to know just what is excluded and what not. Past and future, for example, conceptually separated by the cut to which we give the name of present, and defined as being the opposite sides of that cut, are to some extent, however brief, co-present with each other throughout experience. The literally present moment is a verbal supposition, not a position; the only present ever realized concretely being the "passing moment" in which the dying rearward of time and its dawning future forever mix their lights. Say "now" and it *was* even while you say it.[1]

This looks back, be it noted, to the "specious present" of the *Principles of Psychology*, not to the *durée réelle* of the *Données immédiates*. It is not conceivable that, if James had been interested in, or had desired to identify himself with, more than the positive anti-intellectualism and the general temporalistic *tendency* which Bergson exemplified, he would not have paid more attention to the positive and constructive doctrines of Bergson. But these, we have his own word for it, baffled him, and seemed obscure. The one thing that did stand out clearly was the critique of the concept, and the effect of that critique was to reassure James that the road he himself was on was the right one. Similarly Bergson recognizes the existence in James's philosophy of certain contents to which he takes exception. In his introduction to the French version of *Pragmatism,* he writes, after a very sympathetic and illuminating, though, I think, not a very correct, account of James's general metaphysical position, "certain objections can be offered against it [the pragmatic theory of reality] and we ourselves make certain reservations with respect to it."

James and Bergson are at one, then, in their repudiation of intellectualism, in their general temporalism. Are they similarly at one otherwise? No one that has written of the two men but has failed to deny it. M. Ménard in his painstaking and sympathetic summary of James's *Principles of Psychology* finds profound differences in matters psychological; Mr. Pitkin,[1] M. Boutroux,[2] M. Flournoy,[3] each finds significant differences of varying degrees and directions. Bergson, according to Mr. Pitkin, goes the way of the older cosmologists. He repudiates psycho-physics, and refers the mental stream, born of the collision of the *élan vital* with matter, to the underlying purity of both of these, a purity as such unknowable. James is closer to Fechner than to Bergson, in Mr. Pitkin's view. For James, experience is all, each piece of it hanging to the other by its edges, and the whole, self-containing, hanging on nothing. Where Bergson desiderates unknowably pure metaphysical substrata, James requires only directly experienced objects. For Bergson, life transcends experience, for

[1] "James or Bergson or Who Is against Intellect," *Journal of Philosophy, Psychology, and Scientific Methods,* VII, 9, p. 225.

[2] *William James.*

[3] *La philosophie de William James,* Saint Blaise, 1911.

James, experience transcends concepts, and not life but experience is the last word of metaphysics.

M. Boutroux finds that Bergson and James agree that life is prior to intellect, which is for Bergson a secondary formation developed by the exigencies of adaptation to a spatial world. Bergson thus attains from another point of view, and in the interest of other problems, a view analogous to James's. But the two views do not coalesce. For Bergson, "if intellect distorts reality as immediately given, it does so in the interests of practice. For James, if intellectual knowledge is inadequate, it is so because, adapted to the conditions of practice of a purely material sort, it is unpropitious to pure practice, which is the direct action of soul on soul." Besides, intellect is secondary, according to Bergson, because it contains elements that seem to be foreign to the purely intuitive data of consciousness, which is nothing but duration as such disentangled and abstracted from both time and space. "For James it is the richness and complexity, not the abstractions of experience which measure its authenticity."[1]

But M. Flournoy goes farthest of all in his description of the differences between the American thinker and the French:

It is not clear [he writes] how [James] without absolutely reversing himself, could have been able to accept the vigorously monistic conception implied in the *élan vital originel* whence M. Bergson gets the whole universe by divergent evolution. Nothing can be more opposed than such a vision of things to that which James has always had of the universe: a primordial chaos without a trace of unity, or order, or harmony, or law; pure assemblage of separate and independent principles or entities, the upshot of whose chance relations is the organization of a world of growing harmony and union, never, perhaps, to be completed. . . . . This world is just the opposite of the Bergsonian universe, which, starting with an original, harmonious unity, developed by way of a diversifying evolution toward a continually greater dispersion. It would be difficult, then, to conceive two more contrary visions of the course of events than those of James and Bergson, once we abstract from their common conviction . . . . that the reality of becoming, the incessant creation of novelty, is inconceivable to our intellect and must be apprehended directly in the living experience itself.[2]

[1] P. 90.

[2] *La philosophie de William James*, pp. 184–86.

All these enunciations exhibit facets of fact. Altogether the Bergsonian philosophy actually bears the same relation to radical empiricism as does the "new realism." It, too, we shall see, has a dominant compensatory strain. Though it apparently inverts the ancient vision soaring to eternal things, it is no less a *reconstruction* of experience for the sake of desiderated values. Modern life is more awake to action than to peace; the will attains to things the intellect cannot foresee. The spontaneity of action, hence the certainty of attainment, have become dominant desiderates for our own age. To take the free and enduring movement discoverable in our inner life, to erect it into the metaphysical substrate of all being, to distinguish the residuum as mere appearance against the invincible reality of this, thereby unifying the world, giving a weighted warrant to the hoped-for impotence of death and to the "freedom" of man, is to voice the common desire. This Bergson does. His so doing is no less than the erection into a metaphysic, by developing its implications, of *one* of the

data which radical empiricism freshly discovered and newly stressed. In method, hence,
in the conception of truth, in the ultimate
designation of reality—of mind, of matter, of
the relations between them—in the conception
of God, and of the origin and destiny of man,
where James summarizes and describes, Bergson interprets and transmutes; where James
takes experience as it comes, Bergson first
dialectically extricates "reality" and then
derives appearance from it. The one is truly
democratic in his metaphysics, the other, as
someone has well said, goes the way of the older
cosmologists.

Let us now examine the detail of these
differences.

CHAPTER III

THE METHOD OF INTUITION AND THE PRAGMATIC METHOD

I

Metaphysics by its very nature excommunicates the daily life. "Unreal!" it pronounces the whole great teeming world we live in, with its so varied aspects of sunshine and storm and change, its struggles and reconciliations, its menace, joy, dying, and renewal, all that is the warp and woof of our routinal day, all that experience forces us to take account of, and makes the rock and substance of the human spirit. Unreal! mere shadow and appearance, to be resolved and dissipated as vapor by the sun, in the through-shining light of genuine reality that hides beneath, without enmities, without diversity, without struggle, whole, happy, harmonious; knowledge and power and bliss in one—one substance, one matter, one God; of whatever stuff, One!

This is the immemorial challenge of metaphysics to experience, and it is no wonder
that experience throws back the challenge in
the metaphysician's teeth. "Step from your
cloister into the open street," it tells him,
"with its rows of abrupt buildings jutting into
the even sky and piercing black holes in its
milky blue; with its horrent noises from wagons
and trams and factories; with its wayfarers so
intent each on his private business, each so
willing to be heedless of all else, so needful of
heed, of dodging vehicles and persons, of shut-
ting ears to sounds, eyes to sights, lest every
step land him in disaster. Go out into the
sounding street, I say, and grasp its raw, pulsing
immediacies! Then come back and speak if
you can your belief in your own report that all
its compulsive turmoil is mere unreal appearance, that reality is quite another thing, the
very prototype and paragon of your heart's
desire! You cannot, much as you wish it!
You are but a poetic, adventuring Quixote
seeing windmills as giants and convicts as
blameless heroes. Yours is the shadow-world,

not mine. What! All this moil and sweating
of embattled men who seek livelihood at the
hazard of life a mere mask; all these broken
stretches of sky and earth and water a mere
mask, and quite another thing the true face of
reality? Come, Mr. Metaphysician, I wish
to believe your report; it is my dearest desire.
But how shall I know that your reality is not
the most illusory of illusions, the appearance of
appearance? Teach me how you know it.
How do you know that the world of my toils and
my sorrow wherethrough I pass side by side
with friend and foe is mere appearance and this
lovely world of yours the solely real? *How
do you know?*"

"I have seen," says the metaphysician.

"You have seen," experience retorts, "but I,
too, have seen. And my eyes are as good as
yours and look out upon the same world. How
comes it that you perceive one substance where
I perceive an infinite horde of earth, air, sky,
and water, the sun, and the abounding stars?
How comes it that you perceive freedom and
eternity and harmony where I behold necessity,

and time, and things fighting and feeding one upon the other? If you be not mad or a liar, cause me to see what you see."

So experience retorts to the metaphysician's challenge, and with its retort, raises the "problem of knowledge," or method. This is not, be it observed, a problem that exists in its own right, but something secondary and derivative. It supervenes on a *confrontation of assertions* about reality. Where there is no such confrontation, there is no problem of method; without the contradiction of experience by metaphysics, no "epistemology"; without the ordinary disagreements of men about the data of the daily life, no challenge of "How do you know?" Reality being essentially an active struggle of entities for survival, the corroborative security of method becomes an important affair of civilization, and technique comes to seem as momentous as the residuum of life.

Nowhere is this so patent as in philosophy. The metaphysician is constantly affirming of the whole of reality all sorts of traits that the rest of mankind, and particularly fellow-metaphysicians, do not see in it. Consequently, to a philosophical description of reality there speedily becomes attached an account of how reality was discovered. The latter is the "epistemology" of technical philosophy and is the constant accompaniment of metaphysics. Every great metaphysical system, from *P*lato on, carries with it a theory of knowledge, which is all too often falsely substituted for the system. Modern philosophy in particular is given to this substitution and insists on the "priority of epistemology." The habit is due to Kant, who invented and defended the substitution. Kant saw the contradiction between the rationalism of the Continentals and the empiricism of the English, between the logical architectonic of Leibniz and Wolff and the psychological analyses of *H*ume and *H*artley. Therein he beheld a confrontation in which he refused to takes sides without further evidence. So he invented "epistemology," i.e., an account of how each side got its knowledge, to help him in his decision. But he did not decide in favor of either. He decided in favor of his "epistemology." Neither the empiricist nor the rationalist, he held, had any means of knowing what he knew. The mind can know only *how it knows*, not *what it knows*. Philosophy must give up metaphysics.

But metaphysics continued, in spite of this sage conclusion. In fact, Kant himself, by opposing "postulates of practical reason" to "categories of pure reason," continued it, and continued it in accordance with approved metaphysical tradition. For when experience and common-sense challenge the metaphysician, telling him that they look upon the same world as he and know it in the same way, he replies, "No, you do not know it in the same way. There is another way of knowing, which is the true way. Yours is the way of illusion; it yields only appearances, only phenomena. Mine is the way of truth; it yields reality in its essence; and in no way save mine can reality be known."

Now as metaphysical systems do not agree, one with the other, concerning the nature of reality, it is not to be expected that they should agree concerning the way in which it is known. In effect, their metaphysical conclusions are prior to their epistemological premises, for logically it is the nature of the world that determines the nature of knowledge, and not conversely, unless knowing and being are identified, and then it doesn't matter which goes first.   In such case of *esse's* being the same as *percipi,* the metaphysical conclusion that is intended (for example, Berkeley's God) must itself be *percipi* (else it could not be an object of demonstration), and so the conclusion still determines the premise.   The argument from the way-of-knowing to the thing-known is a circular argument, as M. Bergson observes,[1] and the way of knowing is colored by the quality of what it knows.   According to rationalistic metaphysics, reality is to be apprehended by reason, and the ordinary modes of thought and perception are condemned as deficient reason or as unreason.   Voluntarism and sentimetalism supersede reason by will and emotion in supersessions such as *Pascal's* "reasons of the

[1] Cf. Bergson, *Creative Evolution*, pp. 186–93.

heart," so superior to the mind's reason; or as Schelling's incidence of ideal and real in intellectual intuition. Materialism and sensationalism, when they have another way of knowing at all, similarly reduce the way to the thing known, as do the Epicureans and the Stoics. And so on. Abstract the specific metaphysical coloring from the specific epistemology which reveals reality, as opposed to that which reveals appearance, and you find that all epistemologies agree in *identifying the knowing with what is known.*

Materialistic and sensationalistic philosophies do this less obviously than the non-materialistic and rationalistic ones, but still do it none the less. The great tradition of this distinction belongs, however, to the spiritualistic and the absolutist systems. *H*owever wide their diversity otherwise, their unanimity with regard to this matter is as startling as it is significant.

Consider first the system of *P*lato. To him, more than to any other, the compensatory tradition of philosophy owes its method and authority. To him it owes its foremost keen

vision of the dread philosophic abyss between
reality and appearance, to him its first perception of the contrast between the inadequacies
and failures of experience and the perfection
and excellence of the world of ideas. Yes, there
are ideas, excellent, supreme, eternal, and perfect, the prototypes of all that changes and
moves on earth. But how shall the mind of
man know these, how attain in his imper-
fections to their perfection, in his mortality
to their immortality, in his transiency to their
eternity? What do sense or perception or
even dialectic reveal, more than the flux of the
daily life, in its reason and unreason? Nothing:
they cannot discover the Ideas. But if they
cannot, love can. And what is love but the
yearning of a fallen and imperfect thing for its
lost perfection? What is knowledge but a
procession through love back to the heavenly
estate of the Ideas whence the mind fell?
Nay, the mind is not mortal, it is immortal.
Soon or late it recalls in this earthly life the
heavenly majesty it fell from, it yearns to it
from object to object, until, finally, it throws

off its mortality and resumes its immortality. It becomes again, on earth at rare moments, in heaven eternally, one and the same with the eternal realities it at other times only conceived.

That Aristotle should agree with *Plato* is as much to be expected as that he should naturalize the view he participates in. For where *Plato* is rationalistic, Aristotle is empirical; where *Plato* is mystic, Aristotle is rational. Such is not, however, the case with respect to this part of epistemology. *H*ere Aristotle and *Plato* are at one. *D*istinguishing, as his metaphysic does, between matter and form; describing the world as a teleologic progression from the purity of the one to the purity of the other, each in its purity being transcendent to the world; this metaphysic finds that the ordinary means of knowing (which are sensation and thought) can apprehend no more than the intermediacy and mixture that bridges these purities; that they are attached to the body and culminate in death; that they are incapable of grasping the purities of matter and form as such.

*D*o these purities, then, lie beyond man's grasp ? Matter, indeed, does, being purely a privative thing. But for form, which is active, generative, pure purpose, the mind has a faculty. This is the "active intellect," the νοῦς ποιητικός, bound to no physical organ, the one part of us which is immortal, immaterial, eternal; giving life to all else; actual being whose substance is that of the pure form of God; whose possession is self-possession; whose knowledge is self-knowledge.   For in the active intellect, thinker and thought, knower and known, are one and the same.

The identification is still more vivid and lucid in Plotinos. *H*e is worth while dwelling on, for between him and Bergson there exist very striking resemblances, the more significant for the apparent diametricity of the opposition of their views. For Plotinos followed, of course, the *P*latonic tradition, and to its bitter logical end. What the pursuit comes upon, as the Reality of realities, beside which the ideas of *P*lato, the forms of Aristotle, are mere appearance, is the One. Everywhere and nowhere the One is;[1] everywhere as the cause of all things, nowhere as their Other, their *Different*. Its supremacy lies not in magnitude, for magnitude is beneath it; its supremacy is *potency*, self-sufficiency, self-contained and *unreflective*. "That alone neither knows, nor has what it does not know, but being One present to itself needs not thought of itself."[2] It is all beings because all emanate from it and it generates the thought that is no other than being. To behold it is "intellectual love," a love infinite, the sole true way of knowing. For even as there is a progression between the one and the many, a falling-away from the fulness of Being, so there is a progression of knowledge, a re-ascension unto this fulness, over sense first, then over opinion, over discursive reason, over dialectic, finally over that intuitive knowledge of the "intelligible essence" which is the God of Aristotle, until at last the soul has attained to

[1] Cf. Bergson, *Creative Evolution*, pp. 171-72.
[2] Cf. *Enn.* vi.

"intellectual love."[1]   For the One transcends cognition, even in Aristotle's intuitive way. Such cognition is still relative, and the One is absolute.   To behold it is to *be* it, unreflectively.   The vision of the One dawns upon the soul and absorbs it, a thing beyond utterance, "ineffable."[2]   Subject of language, language can express; and not it alone, but the matters of immediate experience and of intellect. *H*ence, these can only lead the soul to its vision of the great Subject, to the fulness of the ineffable Unity wherein seer and seen are one and indivisible and nothing remains to utter.

It is a similar thing that *D*ante indicates in his supreme statement of that high Thomian beatitude, the *visio divinae essentiae,*[3] so unutterable, and so fecund a source of the mediaeval dialectic of Eckhardt, of Bernard, and of the less sophisticated utterances of Boehme.

---

[1] Cf. Bergson, *Introduction à la métaphysique.*

[2] Cf. H. M. Sheffer, "Ineffable Philosophies," *Journal of Philosophy, Psychology, and Scientific Methods,* VI, 5, p. 123.

[3] Cf. also X. Moisant, "Dieu dans la philosophie de M. Bergson," *Revue de philosophie,* VI (1905).

. . . . My sight, becoming purified, now more and more was entering through the ray of the deep light which of itself is true. From this moment my vision was more potent than our discourse, which faileth before such seeing; and memory faileth before so great violence. As is he, who dreaming, seeth, and when the dream has vanished there remains only the passion's stamp, and no thing else cometh to mind again, even such am I. For almost wholly faileth me my vision, yet doth the sweetness that was born of it still drip within my heart. So doth the snow unstamp itself unto the sun. So the oracles of the Sybil lost themselves in light leaves unto the wind. . . . . I remember that I was the bolder so well to sustain it, as to have united my gazing with the Infinite Worth! O grace abounding, wherein I presumed to fix my look on the eternal light so long that I consumed my sight thereon. . . . .[1]

*H*ere, as earlier, there is an *elimination of differences;* the realm of grace is attained by a vision and deification, in an ecstasy wherein, as St. Bernard says, the individual is merged in the divine eternal essence "as a drop of water in a cask of wine."

The aspects in which the *amor intellectus dei* of Spinoza differs from this constitute an almost corporate identity with the characteristics of

[1] *Paradiso*, xxxiii, 52–84.

Bergsonian intuition. God and substance, Nature, the One, the All, these are but names, according to Spinoza, for the interpenetrating identity of infinite attributes or qualities, each infinitely vast. Of these, two are known to man, the extension of matter, the intension of thought. Less than the whole, they are mere appearance, bare phenomena; yet because they are flesh of its flesh and blood of its blood, they are true expressions of it, in so far forth. But not in their immediacy, nor in their character as knowledge in sensation, in perception, in imagination. As such they give rise to ideas which are unclear, indistinct, inadequate; ideas by nature the essence of error and knowers of mere appearance. The One is to be known and possessed in another way, the way of adequacy. Therein the order of perception and the order of reality are one and the same. The whole world is perceived *genetically*, things in their essence and with their causes; and perceived in one free act. Our power to perceive is our virtue, our virtue is but our effort to preserve our selfhood, our selfhood is *Divinity*.

In the recognition of our essential identity with
God lies our happiness and our immortality.
Now this recognition comes in intuition. It
is "the intellectual love of God"; it is the death
of the difference between God and soul, substance and mode, man and nature. It is the
point in which the boundless universe is
gathered up; all interpenetrates and is one.
We see God because we *are* God, and our love
toward him is no other than his love toward
himself. In his humanity, then, man con-
centrates and realizes the boundless energy of
creative nature (*natura naturans*) and estab-
lishes his being forever.

II

Few systems could be more essentially various in their background, outlook, and approach
than those here reviewed. The moralism of
Plato and Aristotle, the mystic transcendentalism of Plotinos, the salvational supernaturalism
of the mediaevals, and the confident naturalism
of Spinoza, all these express tendencies inwardly
diverse in both origin and quality. Yet their

outcome, with respect to the way of knowing metaphysical reality, whatever character that has, is startlingly the same. Call it "intuition," "intellectual love of God," "beatitude," "intellectual sympathy," what you will. Beside it all other modes of knowing are false and relative. It alone is true and absolute. Yet it depends upon them and cannot be without them. From sensation to dialectic, those modes constitute the stages that of necessity lead to it. If it supersedes them, it also presupposes them. In each case it consists essentially in the *identification of the knower with the thing known.*

Such an identification, related to other forms of knowing in the historic fashion, is also the method of Bergson. With respect to the knowing of metaphysical reality, Bergson belongs to the philosophic tradition. For him also there is a true way and a false way of knowing, a way absolute and a relative way. For him also truth is a thing primary and ultimate, not a thing derivative and functional. But whereas, in the tradition of metaphysics, epistemology argues in a circle, unaware, from the thing to be known to the mode of knowing, Bergson does so knowingly and with intention.[1] Metaphysical reality, he teaches, is life in its onrush, pure duration. Whatever is unvital, static, motionless, is appearance, an inversion of the real. Now the independent epistemological tradition, particularly in the work of its founder, Kant, is concerned alone with this inversion. Kant presumes the unity and universality of the scientific method. But science turns on laws, on relations, and a relation is nothing apart from the intellect which relates. Science must assume therefore in its totality a merely "relative and human character." This it does under the Kantian treatment—and must—for Kant completely misses the fact that science becomes more and more symbolical as it passes "from the physical to the vital, from the vital to the psychical." To him all experience is *one* and is the experience which our intellect constructs. All this, Bergson thinks, is based on the fundamentally false

[1] Cf. *Creative Evolution*, trans. by Mitchell, pp. 178 ff.

assumption that the vital can be apprehended intellectually, that life in its proper direction can be perceived by its inversion. God and freedom and perhaps immortality, which are beyond demonstration by the intellect and its constructions, may be, hence, quite within the grasp of the *other* way of knowing.[1]   This other way of knowing is intuition, not postulation of the practical reason. Bergson, it is to be observed, is bolder than Kant and goes the way of the older metaphysics.   He reconverts the postulate into the dogma.

By "intuition" Bergson designates "that kind of intellectual sympathy by which one sets oneself in the interior of an object in order to coincide with the very reality of that object, with its uniqueness, with that in it, consequently, which cannot be expressed."[2]   The knowledge so attained is absolute, inasmuch as mind and object coincide.   In this coincidence the "point of view" disappears.   The

[1] Cf. *op. cit.*, pp. 356–63.

[2] "Introduction à la métaphysique," *Revue de métaphysique et morale* (1903).

whole object is apprehended at once, in its innermost reality, its perfection, its infinity, its simplicity. Symbolize, analyze, and you shatter this simple intuition; absolute knowledge gives way to relative knowledge; "points of view" become important. All you attain with your symbols and analyses, however, is merely the bringing to terms of the unknown with the known, the generation of an infinite collection of predicates that are intended to bring back a unique and simple subject, and that can never, never attain this original unique unity of interpenetrating qualities in which each is all and all are each. *P*redicates are images, or concepts, and neither can represent this heterogeneous unity. It transcends representation: to know it you must become it. But science is representation, an arrangement of conceptual notes, which, however cleverly taken, cannot reproduce their subject-matter. Reality therefore transcends also science. Science is not really empirical. "A true empiricism is one that sets itself the task of getting as close as possible to the original itself, of sounding the depths of its life, of feeling the pulses of its spirit by a sort of *intellectual auscultation.* Such an empiricism is the true metaphysics."[1]

What is this *auscultation intellectuelle?* It is the supersession, in the *P*lotinian way, of dialectic, of science, of all conceptual knowledge, by intuition. Concepts and analyses are born of our insufficiency. We piece out and extend our senses and consciousness with activities no longer perceptive, "activities of abstraction, generalization, and reasoning." These activities are not creative but ordinative, ignoring more than they handle, and contradicting each other continually. But suppose now that instead of seeking to transcend perception, we sink ourselves in it, developing and expanding it. "Suppose we set our will in it, and this will, dilating, dilates our vision of reality. Like the artist, then, we shall have subordinated our faculty of doing to our faculty of knowing.[2]" The exigencies of life require us to act, to con-

[1] *Op. cit.*, p. 14.
[2] *La perception du changement*, p. 13.

ceptualize, to reason.   The concepts we attain
to go in couples are contradictory.   Neither
one nor both can lead back to the intuition
from which practical necessity draws them,
though that intuition can make clear how both
spring from it.   Each concept is only a practical question that our activity puts to reality,
and that the latter replies to with yes or no,
thus permitting the very essence of this reality
to escape.   To get to that, the mind must
practice an inversion, an inversion in analysis
itself.   Modern mathematics does so when
it substitutes the making for the made and
aims at recovering the generative conceptions
of magnitude.   Science does so when it makes
use of ideas "where clearness is at bottom
nothing more than the once attained assurance
of their profitable manipulation, where truth
and fertility are so many encounters with reality that do not necessarily converge toward one
centre."[2]   With these concepts a long famili-
arity is needful.   "It is impossible to have an
intuition of reality, that is, an intellectual

Introduction à la métaphysique, p. 34.

sympathy with its innermost nature unless its confidence has been won by long comradeship with its external manifestations." Once won, these manifestations will integrate in intuition, and yield the reality that underlies. The object of metaphysics is by their means "to effect (*opérer*) qualitative differentiations and integrations." So, however, metaphysics presupposes science and continues it, although superseding it. For metaphysics is a universal science, and science too often but a relative and symbolic knowledge, in terms of pre-existing concepts which aim to pass from the static to the dynamic. Whereas metaphysics must needs be that "intuitive knowledge which installs itself in movement as such and adopts the very life of things." In this installation, which is intuition, science and philosophy unite, and the latter continues and fulfils no less than it supersedes the former.

Still more explicitly *P*lotinian is the account of the relation between science and intuition which Bergson gives in *Creative Evolution*. Since, for him, epistemology and metaphysics

reciprocally imply each other, a theory of reality
is at one and the same time a theory of knowledge, a theory of life, a theory of instinct, and
of intellect. Evolutionally, hence, intuition
attaches itself to instinct, analysis to intellect.
Instinct is synthetic and knows a much-at-
once; intellect is analytic and knows one concept. Instinct is knowledge of the substance of
reality; intellect only of its form. But because
instinct is knowledge of substance, it is limited
in its scope; and because intellect is knowledge
of form, it is confined only to appearances.
The one, by itself, is non-speculative, the other
volatile. *H*ence "there are things that intelligence alone is able to seek, but which left to itself it will never find. These things instinct
alone could find; but it will never seek them."[1]
It follows that neither intellect nor instinct can
by itself alone be the philosophical way of
knowing. "*Philosophy*," says Bergson, almost
in the words of Plotinos, "can only be an effort
to dissolve again into the Whole."[2] The whole
of reality can be known only by the whole of

---

[1] *Creative Evolution*, p. 151.   [2] *Ibid.*, p. 191.

mind.   Now the whole of mind is intuition, and intuition is instinct *and* intellect, "instinct that has become disinterested, self-conscious, capable of reflecting upon its object and enlarging it indefinitely."[1]   Instinct is sympathy, and instinct, so changed, is *intellectual sympathy*. It is then identical with the very substance and flow of reality itself.   The two diverse and. opposed movements of the mind have, in it, been dissolved and united into their original durative force and are one with each other and with the whole metaphysical onrush, with that which is pure duration, consciousness, life. Thus philosophy follows science.   It superposes upon the latter's analytic and symbolic knowledge another kind.   It reintegrates our scientific formulae into "absolute knowledge," and "in the absolute we live and move and have our being."   This absolute knowledge "is reality itself, in the profoundest meaning of the word, that we reach by the combined and progressive development of science and philosophy."   But this is very different from

[1] *Op. cit.*, p. 176.

a synthesis of the material or intellectual or scientific knowledge which is the means of attaining it. It is an *expérience intégral*, but it is not a generalization of experience; it is absolutely non-discursive and unthinking, for like the *P*lotinian intuition of the One, it dissolves discourse into its dynamic origins and transmutes thought into transcendental feeling.

This knowledge-and-reality admits of degrees, from the absolute coincidence of the self with itself, to matter, in which there is the minimum of duration.

Install yourself in duration by means of intuition, and you "have first of all the feeling of a very specific tension, whose very specificity appears like a choice from among an infinity of possible durations. You perceive present as many durations as you will, all very different from one another, although each of them, reduced to concepts, i.e., envisaged from without from opposite points of view, leads always back to the same indefinable combination of the many and the one.[1]

Now in real time we do not logically need to suppose any *real* duration other than our own, just as there might not exist any other color

[1] *Introduction à la métaphysique*, pp. 23 ff.

than orange. But even as intuition feels in orange a tendency to *red* and to *yellow*, prolonged perhaps in the whole spectrum between these two, so *our* intuition of our own duration brings us into contact with a continuity of durations which we should follow, whether up or down; in both cases we may expand indefinitely by a more and more violent effort; in both cases we may transcend ourselves. Going downward we subdivide, spatialize, till we pass from quality to quantity; finally reaching pure *repetition*. By pure repetition materiality is defined. In the upward direction duration *grows*, its limit being eternity.

Not conceptual eternity, ... but a living and ever-moving eternity, where we find our own duration as vibrations are found in light,[1] which is the concretion of all durations just as matter is its deglutition. Intuition moves between these two extreme limits and this movement is metaphysics itself.

To become metaphysical, Bergson tells us, the mind must cease to be practical. For him, as for historical philosophy, action is the enemy of vision; the faculty of speculation, the artist's

---

[1] The favorite simile of Plotinos.

faculty which perceives reality in its go, is independent of that of action and may be detached from it; the intuition of reality is, indeed, the antithesis of its control. Control is needful and utility arises only when there is an *other*, a something *not* ourselves, that may make for righteousness but does not make for peace. Intelligence and analysis are the method and form of control. They are contingent on this *other*, and are, with it, hence, only derivative and secondary. Intuition abolishes otherness; in it the thinker and the thought are one. The spirit ceases to act and lets itself live. It then becomes identical with the universe, and the universe, it is well known, need adapt itself to nothing. The universe is absolute, its being is one and the same as its knowing. The knowing, hence, is absolute. Now, inasmuch as the procedure of the sciences and the arts applies always to an *other*, is only the method whereby *homo faber* renders the world more congenial to himself, that kind of knowing which is the substance of the arts and the sciences must be of a genus quite other than intuition, and can apprehend only appearance. In this conclusion, Bergson agrees with the philosophic tradition, from *Plato* to Spinoza. *He* does not agree with William James.

He does not agree with William James because the latter, in pragmatism, does not aim to distinguish the method of philosophy from that science, but to extend the method of science to philosophy.[1] For pragmatism, the instrument in its works does not conceal reality; it reveals reality. For pragmatism the fallacy of thought lies in the hypostasis of the instrument, and not in its use; for Bergson it lies in use as such. The distinction is fundamental, for this reason: Bergson derives his epistemology from his metaphysics, and is compelled thereby to give his epistemology an especial twist; pragmatism observes knowing and method as so many empirical data of expe-

[1] "Since philosophers are only men thinking about things in the most comprehensive possible way, they can use any method whatsoever freely. Philosophy must, in any case, complete the sciences and must incorporate their methods. One cannot see why, if such a policy should appear advisable, philosophy might not end by forswearing all dogmatism whatever, and become as hypothetical in her manner as the most empirical science of them all."—*Some Problems of Philosophy*, pp. 25–26.

rience, neither better nor worse than any of the others, and studies them as they occur.

Intuition is not one of such epistemological occurrences. It has its basis, like all hypostases, in fact of some kind, of course; but it becomes what Bergson describes it to be only by hypostatizing this basis. The historic glorification of intuition is nothing more than a hypostasis of the instrument. A description of how this particular hypostasis arises will be at one and the same time a description of the difference between the pragmatic method and the method of intuition.

III

Pragmatism asserts that "the meaning of any proposition can always be brought down to some particular consequence in our future practical experience, ... the point lying in the fact that the experience must be particular rather than in the fact that it must be active."[1] This particularity applies to every possible content of experience—concepts,

[1] *The Meaning of Truth*, p. 210.

of the instrument and not its use / Bergson -> USE

percepts, relations, time, space, mind, what you will—in such wise that "the parts of experience hold together from next to next by relations that are themselves parts of experience.[1]   The directly apprehended universe needs, in short, no extraneous transempirical connective support, but possesses in its own right a concatenated or continuous structure."   Nothing, consequently, is excluded from immediacy.   Every item, from the most solid to the most ephemeral of the daily life, with its shocks and pains and resistances and evil, occurs in that flow with all its intrinsic nature knowable.   In so far forth, Bergson's immediacy excludes these items: it is perfect and continuous and harmonious; James's includes every possible entity that the mind can think.   And the knowledge of any such entity in its immediacy, James calls *knowledge-of-acquaintance*.

Like intuition, this knowledge apprehends its object in its uniqueness, but unlike intuition, it is not an identification of self, or mind,

[1] *A Pluralistic Universe*, p. 280; cf. *The Will to Believe*, p. 278; *Essays in Radical Empiricism*, pp. 16-20.

and object.   The mind terminates in the object, as your mind and my mind terminate in these words that I write and you read, but mind and object are not one.   "All the *whats* as well as the *thats* of reality, relational as well as terminal, are in the end content of immediate concrete perception."[1]   Now, if the immediate were actually perfect and continuous, as Bergson says it is, it could never complicate itself into representative and conceptual knowledge; the mind would rest in it as the gods rest in the eternal ideas, or Bergson in his intuition, without seeking or desiring anything else.   But the immediate directly compels us to like and to dislike.   It is not throughout propitious. The mind flees from or seeks to destroy its enemies and clings to and seeks to conserve its friends.   It prefers the continuous and the perfect and rejects the shocking and the evil. These responses to the immediate, which bear the same relation to it as the waves of the sea to the sea, give rise to what is called *mediate* or reflective knowledge, the kind of knowledge

[1] *A Pluralistic Universe*, p. 342, note.

which James calls *knowledge-about.* The pragmatic rule is a rigorous statement of the empirical processes by which *knowledge-about* arises
and gets reduced again to *knowledge-of-acquaintance.* It explains the nature of *meaning* and
the nature of *truth.*

The distinction here made is a distinction
analogous to that of Bergson's between intuitive and conceptual knowledge. But for Bergson this distinction is one of *kind;* for James it
is one of degree. Knowledge-about is not the
inversion or opposite of knowledge-of-acquaintance. It is the complication of such knowledge
as a wave is the special complication of the sea.
Knowledge-of-acquaintance became knowledge-
about by way of addition, not by way of sub-
traction or opposition, and its cognitive utility
is absolutely contingent on its retaining its
status in immediacy. What are the reasons
for this?

The first is, that unless any piece of *knowledge-about* lead to and dissolve in *that* which
it is about, it is not knowledge at all, but fact.
Now its leading or pointing is what James calls

ambulatory, not saltatory; it proceeds by a "concatenated" movement from next to next, and every step in this movement is matter of direct or immediate experience. For example, I think, as I write, of a book in the next room, to which I wish to refer. My thought, as I now think it, is *of* and *about* the book. Of what does the thought consist? Of a vague visual image of the book's shape and color, of kinaesthetic tendencies in my limbs, in the biceps of my left hand, and in the muscles at the back of my neck, and of a well-defined *feeling of direction* which seems different from these kinaesthetic sensations but which determines, localizes, and integrates them. They form a sort of hole, very specific and definite, in which only one thing can fit. And their total effect is that of a specific impulsion toward that thing. Of all this, and the unrest which accompanies it, I have immediate cognition. It is all matter of acquaintance. Now suppose that I relax my attention from my writing. I find that I rise from the table, pass into the next room to the bookshelf, pick up one book, then another, then another, finally stop. The stopping is not a change of action into inaction. I do not feel inactive. I feel a different direction of action, an action which does not seem to contain any unrest. The book I now hold in my hand *fits*. It fulfils or satisfies the tendency. The visual image is gone, the particular sense of direction is gone, the whole has melted into the tactile and visual sensations of the book and the sense of poise, of satisfaction. No step in this movement but has been immediately felt in its substance and in its relations. And the transition from the first to the last step has at all points been as much matter of acquaintance as either terminus—*a quo* or *ad quem*. The *terminus a quo*, however, has been called *knowledge-about* the *terminus ad quem*, an *idea* of the book. What is it that turns this object into an idea, into a representation of another thing, into something that has *meaning?* Empirically it is nothing more than the immediately felt motricity, the feeling of direction, added to the visual and other "images." This is the particular element that gives *meaning* to objects of direct apprehension, that causes them to be *about* an object, between which and the mind they are the *mean*. This is the element that most disappears when the *meaning* terminates in the *meant*. The rest smoothly adds itself to, and is fulfilled in, the object. I pause when I get the right book. I can no longer distinguish the visual image from this book, although I did distinguish it from the others that I handled, and so on. My idea of the book has been true, my meaning correct, because the movement it initiated in the direction it took culminated in satisfaction. It was *felt* as substitutional, as reaching beyond itself. Without this feeling, which is an immediate cognition of inner tendency and direction, "idea" is just so much flat fact, with no meaning, unless it be said to mean itself.[1]

Well, having the book in hand, how do I know it as *the* book, the goal and terminus of the cognitive movement unrolled in time? First of all, *that* movement is gone. Its place

[1] Cf. *Essays in Radical Empiricism*, pp. 67–90.

has been taken by what can best be described as a glow of direct possession. There has occurred, at the same time, an intensification and enrichment of the spatial and color complexes which were the substantive parts of the "idea." In their paler rôle, they were "mental"; now I cannot distinguish them from the total "book" into which they seem indissolubly merged. They have not been less immediate or real than the book now is, but less adequate and satisfactory. If, now, I am a traditional metaphysician, I call them "appearance," and that fulfilment of them which I designate by the word "book" I call reality. They are "concept," that "percept"; they are relative, that absolute. The knowledge of them, furthermore, I distinguish similarly; as ideational, as meaning, it is merely analytic, conceptually relative; as *meant*, as satisfaction, it is absolute, it is coincidence of self and object in intuition. Empirically, however, there is no such dichotomy. The cognitive immediacy is *the same* in the whole process from beginning to end. It is the percept's retroactive validating power that certifies me as an actual knower of the book. "Our fields of experience," as James says, "have no more definite boundaries than have our fields of view. Both are fringed with a *more* that continuously develops and that continuously supersedes them as life succeeds."[1] Immediacy of every datum in a cognitive experience is the *conditio sine qua non* of the experience's being cognitive. An unexperienced *meaning* is not a meaning.

In point of fact, every piece of knowledge-of-acquaintance becomes in its turn knowledge-about without thereby forfeiting its status in immediacy. Concept and percept are consubstantial and interchangeable, differing not in nature but in function. Traditional metaphysics, however, hypostatizes the *function,*[2]

---

[1] *Essays in Radical Empiricism*, p. 71.

[2] In this wise Bergson, for example, hypostatizes duration. Finding it, as a matter of acquaintance, directly satisfactory, and coupling with it the compensatory values of "freedom" and "unity," he declares it knowable only intuitively and rules out its "conceptual" or representative use as impossible. Duration, his thesis runs, cannot be used instrumentally; it is always a *meant*, a cognitive *terminus ad quem*, never a *terminus a quo*. But pragmatism denies this. The pragmatist points out that any entity we experience directly can have the function of leading

and, observing that the cognitive satisfaction resides in knowledge-of-acquaintance, dubs such knowledge intuition, identifies in it mind and object, and makes it the key to reality.

Bergson → true knowledge ≠ Useful knowledge

IV

This hypostasis has important bearing on the further consideration of method which is involved in the conception of truth. In *Matter and Memory*, Bergson speaks[1] of "distinguishing the point of view of customary or useful knowledge from that of true knowledge." And in his introduction to the French version of *Pragmatism*, he speaks of James as believing that truth is created by human imagination.

We invent truth in order to make use of reality, just as we create mechanical converters for the utilization of natural forces. The essence of the pragmatic to and meaning. The perception of duration is not exempt. Whenever we use it as a qualifying predicate, it has that function, as, e.g., in "Man endures." It is futile to retort that such a use conceptualizes it; for if it be not a concept by its nature, use will not make it so, since use is additive—function to substance, so to speak. And, in any event, concepts are as much matters of acquaintance as percepts, and their cognitive use is an enrichment of their immediacy, not an abrogation thereof.

[1] P. 243.

James → truth is created by human imagination

conception of truth might, to my mind, be summed up with some such formula as this: while for other theories a new truth is a discovery, for pragmatism such a truth is an invention.[1]

Although he recognizes that this analogy and these terms are not James's, M. Bergson thinks them faithful to the spirit of James's system, and most in harmony with his theory of reality, and with respect to that Bergson himself "would make . . . . certain reservations."[2]   With these reservations we shall have to deal in another place.   It is sufficient here merely to mention them in order to indicate that if made with respect to the pragmatic theory of reality, analogous reservations must be made with respect to the pragmatic definition of truth. What are they? Bergson does not say in so many words, but that they must needs be radical is evinced by his sharp contrast between "useful knowledge" and "true knowledge." It is of the spirit of the Bergsonian philosophy that the true shall be the opposite of the useful, while for pragmatism

[1] *Le pragmatisme*, Introduction, p. 11.

[2] Ibid., p. 25.

Insight begins ability to love someon... [handwritten]

the very essence of truth is utility. Utility
abolishes insight according to Bergson; according to James, without utility, insight can have
no meaning.   Bergson ⇒ Utility abolishes insight [handwritten]

The key to this contrast is the radical metaphysical divorce that Bergson compels between
conceptual or discursive and intuitive knowledge.   In the beginning man and nature are
one; "in the absolute we live and move and
have our being."   But the needs of existence
compel us to separate ourselves from the whole
to which we belong, to view and to treat it as
another.   These views, in sensation, perception,
and intellection, are in a *different dimension*
from the reality itself.   They are mere views,
snapshots, cinematographic instants, cognitive
cuts of something that is itself not plural but
one, not discrete but continuous.   Our views,
hence, serve our needs, and help us to control
the reality we view.   But in this service they
are truer to *our* nature than to that of reality.
Their utility forms a thick veil between us and
it, distorts its character, and belies its nature.
These can be revealed only in intuition.   Utility

is vociferous, intuition is silent. Utility is symbolic, plural, discursive, and always relative; intuition is identical with the object itself, is *one*, dumb, absolute, ineffable. Intuition, hence, is truth; utility, mere falsification. If you wish to know a thing truly, you must be that thing.

Also with respect to truth, then, Bergson belongs to the philosophic tradition. In that tradition, what is truth is a property of the object of belief, not of the belief. The truth of a belief belongs to it in virtue of a quality in an alien thing, and if once true, it is true forever. *H*ence, the absolute alone, or God, to whom all things are *immediately present*, who is thinker and thought in one, can possess truth, and the human mind must depend on its coincidence with this supernal mind for its own poor fragments and shreds of truth. The same essential identity of thinker and thought are demanded in the Bergsonian conception of truth. Truth is an absolute, a possession, not a use. It belongs to the intellect when it apprehends space and matter, to the soul when it apprehends movement and life. For then these apprehend only what they are.

The pragmatist, coming to his investigation of knowledge without preconceptions and without prejudices, treating knowledge as just another empirical item of experience, to be dealt with on its own account, sees truth in exactly the inverse way. For the pragmatist, truth is what we live by, not what we rest in. We rest in the immediate, and, as the discussion of method has made clear, everything is immediate, concepts, percepts, evil, good, things, imaginations, realities, illusions; no item of experience can be an item without being immediate. If, then, we are to distinguish between truth and error, immediacy cannot help us, and intuition, we have seen, is no more than a designation for a *particular use of satisfactory immediacies*. Truth must be something super-added to the plain immediacy of any content of cognition. Be that content simple or complex, it becomes true when there occurs, together with its other qualities, one more of specific and recognizable nature. What is

this one more *known as?* How is a content
of experience as *true* different from a content
of experience as *fact?* The difference lies in
that the former works. Fact, the immediate,
is silent; truth has a voice. Already in 1884,
William James had pointed out this difference.
It is the difference between "knowledge-
of-acquaintance" and "knowledge-about."
Knowledge-of-acquaintance is dumb, without
being ineffable. The mind holds the thing
it is acquainted with in a specific immediate
feeling, the feeling of *that* fact in its uniqueness.
But as such, the thing can offer no deliverance
about anything, not even about itself. It is
neither true nor false, but is genuinely absolute. To become true or false, it must get
into relation; it must operate and signify.
Suppose, e.g.,

some little feeling that gives a *what.* If other feelings
should succeed which remember the first, its *what* may
stand as subject or predicate of some piece of knowledge-about, of some judgment, perceiving relations
between it and other *whats* which the other feelings
may know. The hitherto dumb *q* [i.e., the feeling-
content] will then receive a name and be no longer

speechless. But every name, as students of logic know, has its "denotation," and the denotation always means some reality or content, relationless *ab extra* or with its internal relations unanalyzed. . . . . No relation-expressing proposition is possible except on the basis of a preliminary acquaintance with such "facts," with such contents as this. Let *q* be fragrance, let it be toothache, or let it be a more complex kind of feeling, like that of the full moon swimming in her blue abyss: it must first come in that simple shape and be held fast in that first intention, before any knowledge *about* it can be attained. The knowledge *about* it is *it* with a context added. Undo *it*, and what is added cannot be context.[1]

*H*ence, truth, if it be a deliverance at all, and have articulation, must be attributed to the *context*, not to the text—that is, if by truth we mean what has always been meant, a *quality* of *thinking*, not of mere fact. As a quality of thinking, truth is (and error no less) that which turns the *immediate* into the *mediate*. It makes knowledge-of-acquaintance over into knowledge-about. And the truth or error of knowledge-about is identical with its prosperous or its unsuccessful *workings*. These workings are the concrete, immediately-experienced

[1] *The Meaning of Truth*, pp. 14, 15.

transitions from the knowledge-about to that which the knowledge *is* about. They partake of what is for Bergson the intrinsic and underlying character of reality itself, since they are *transitions*, are *actions*, are the very force of cognition. But they are cognitive not because they are not related. They are cognitive because they are related. Cognition is relation, even in knowledge-of-acquaintance. And so far as only action and transition are reality, relation is reality. And the cognition present in predication, in judgment, in every form of knowledge-about is true in so far as the relations it initiates progress harmoniously to their mergence in direct conjunction with the object of their interest.

Use, it follows, M. Bergson to the contrary notwithstanding, does not veil, but reveals, reality. Truth *is* the *revelation*, the uncovering, and even the *creation*, of one reality by means of another, and it is even the identification of one reality with another. Truth is prosperous cognitive instrumentation, under any and all of these conditions. When, therefore, James

speaks of vicious intellectualism, of the falsi-
fying effect of concepts, of the "opposition"
between the conceptual and the real, he does
not mean what Bergson means. He means
exactly the opposite thing. Bergson's presuppositions are metaphysical. *He* finds concepts to belong to a metaphysical order of being
utterly different from that of reality.   They are
alien to it and are born only by aborting it;
they express in use our needs, our practical
interests, and all those qualities which are not
the interests of reality. James has no such
presuppositions. *P*ercepts and concepts are
"consubstantial."   They are of the same, not
of different, orders of being. They interact,
and work on each other in a variety of ways.
Concepts, being easier to handle, are more
naturally the furniture and tools of intellection than percepts. We substitute one for
the other *in use*, and interchangeably.   In use,
and only so long as in this use, in the exercise
of *instrumental function*, concepts and all that
they imply are true to each other, analysis is
valid, and falsification is impossible.   Abandon

the use, and analysis becomes inevitably falsi-fication. Why? Because a *functional* use is converted into a metaphysical one; knowledge-*about*, *qua* about, is identified with knowledge-of-acquaintance; context is treated as if it were text. And this is falsification. It is no less an error than would be the action of a thirsty man who, having discovered that water can be made from hydrogen and oxygen, tries to quench his thirst by swallowing quantities of these gases. A similar activity constitutes in discourse what James means by vicious intellectualism and abstractionism. Now James enthusiastically agrees with Bergson that the metaphysical substitution of one reality for another is falsi-fication;[1] he does not agree that the cognitive substitution is such. Thus, for Bergson, hydro-gen and oxygen would belong to an altogether different metaphysical order from water; and consequently the *cognitive use* of these gases as knowledge-*about* water becomes error. For James, on the other hand, the liquid and the two gases are on the same metaphysical level;

[1] Cf. *A Pluralistic Universe*, chap. v.

the cognitive use of one with respect to the other is quite correct, and the only error is the *hypostatization* of *cognitive* or functional identity into metaphysical identity—it is drinking gases instead of water.

We conceive a concrete situation by singling out some salient or important feature in it, and classing it under that; then, instead of adding to its previous characters all the positive consequences which the new way of conceiving it may bring, we proceed to use our concept privatively; we reduce the originally rich phenomenon to the naked suggestions of that value abstractly taken, treating it as a case of "nothing but" that concept, and acting as if all the other characters from which the concept is abstracted were expunged.[1]

For James, hence, falsification belongs to the realm of metaphysics; for Bergson, to the realm of cognition. And since, for both, cognition is ordinarily understood as of utilitarian origin and character, utility becomes identical with unreality for the one and with truth for the other. But in point of fact, Bergson hypostatizes truth. *He* makes the confusion common to all critics of pragmatism and transfers the eulogium which derives from use in

---

[1] *The Meaning of Truth*, p. 249.

knowledge-about, to the outcome of use, to knowledge-of-acquaintance. For Bergson substitutes fact, which simply is, without either truth or falsehood, for knowledge which has one or the other of these attributes according to its behavior.

For the pragmatist true knowledge is knowledge-*about*. And it remains true only so long as it is *about*. Knowledge-of-acquaintance makes no deliverance. The only thing it reveals is itself, and when it is pretended that it can reveal, in its intentless and dimensionless *immediacy*, anything other than itself, that pretense is falsification.[1] But when an object of acquaintance is put to work, when it is manipulated as a means of control of *other* objects of acquaintance, to point to them, to clear the way for them, to *act* in their place, it in so far forth helps to reveal them, not by masquerading in their shape, but by clearing out everything that might stand in the way (including itself) of their self-revelation. When it does so, it is

[1] Cf. my earlier discussion of this point "James, Bergson, and Mr. Pitkin," *Journal of Philosophy, Psychology, and Scientific Methods*, VII, 13, p. 353.

true, and only then. Its behavior is then a harmonious transition from one piece of knowledge-of-acquaintance to another different from the first, and enriched by the transition. Representatively "to know an object is . . . . to . . . . lead to it through a context which the world supplies. To know an object immediately . . . . or intuitively is for mental content and object to be identical, i.e., for object to be apprehended without intermediaries or context."[1]   And that is the whole story.

[1] *The Meaning of Truth,* pp. 46, 50.

CHAPTER IV

THE REVELATIONS OF INTUITION AND THE DISCOVERIES OF PRAGMATISM

I

Since epistemology and the doctrine of method are inevitably circular, making use, in their very construction, ot exactly those materials of reality which are to be apprehended and defined by their application, to discuss the theory of knowledge or method is to discuss its implied metaphysic, and to apply either or both is to apprehend the metaphysical soil from which they spring and the experiential atmosphere they grow in. This we saw in the last chapter. Intuition could be defined only by means of what it exhibits, the pragmatic method only in terms of that to which it applies. It is now needful to look more deeply into the revelations of intuition and the discoveries of pragmatism, to study in and for themselves their nature and inward constitution, to see clearly and distinctly their similarities and differences, and to apprehend the bearing of their traits on the destiny of man and the rule of good.

Methodologically, no two devices could differ more completely than that of James and that of Bergson. And, in spite of a certain identity of spirit and direction, of sympathetic appreciation of each other, the difference shows itself as still more pervasive and more profound, metaphysically. *P*aradoxical as it may seem, Bergson is before all things systematic, consistently architectonic, a monist who insists on an irrefragable difference between appearance and reality; a logician who with rigorous dialectic deduces the character of the one from the nature of the other. James, on the contrary, is before all things intent on insights and data rather than on system. *H*is philosophy is a mosaic, not an architectonic. He does not set out from one intuition which is the womb and matrix of all else. For him there is everywhere a new beginning, and the piecemeal character of knowledge-of-acquaintance is rooted in the plural character of the reality that

Bergson = universe with two orders of the *most*, (monarchist)
James => no order or infinite of orders (democratic) *metaphysics*

it apprehends. Thus, where Bergson beholds a universe, James sees a multiverse; where Bergson envisages at the most two orders, one in any event the derivative and inversion of the other, James perceives no order whatever, or an infinitude of orders, each the peer of the others. The fact is, as has been noted, that James is a democrat in metaphysics. Bergson, on the contrary, is a monarchist. For him the distinction between appearance and reality is aboriginal and final. For James it is secondary and functional. From Bergson's standpoint, James's philosophy must be essentially intellectualistic; from James's, Bergson's philosophy must turn on a hypostasis of the instrument, on the transmutation of a *use* into a substance. Bergson, in a word, belongs here, more than ever, to the philosophic tradition. It is James again who strikes out anew.

Let us consider why and how this is so.

Three qualities, we have seen, mark off the philosophic tradition from radical empiricism. The first is its love of "wholeness" which leads to system-building, and the reconstruction of

the variety and multitudinousness of experience out of a few ultimate and primordial
elements which are "universal" and pervasive.
The second is the designation of all things
which are composed of these elements or are
different from them as *appearance,* to be set
over against their own *reality.* The third is the
assignment to reality of a *compensatory* nature;
the assertion of its homogeneity with human
nature in such wise that human life and
human values are, without any possible risk,
by it somehow conserved forever. Not all
these traits appear simultaneously in each traditional system. Some emphasize one, some
another, but all in the long run, from *P*latonism
to Absolutism, are distinctly marked by them.

Bergson's philosophy is so not less but more,
and his views, as we shall see, show in metaphysics, even as in epistemology, significant
similitudes with great systems in the tradition
—with, for example, that of *P*lato, and that of
Spinoza. True, he does offer profound and
elaborate criticisms of these ·thinkers,[1] but

[1] Cf. *Creative Evolution,* pp. 275–370, trans. by Mitchell.

these criticisms apply rather to generalities of emphasis and to certain verbal differences, than to the concrete detail of vision and to the constructive development of reality from within. In these matters Bergson, at least in *Creative Evolution*, is far closer to *P*lato and Spinoza than he is to William James. For both these older philosophers the daily life is appearance and not reality. For both of them this appearance arises through the *individuation* of the primal reality: according to *P*lato, through the action of the Idea conceived, not as a form, but as a *power*, on non-being, or *space* ($\chi\acute{\omega}\rho\alpha$), so that, though in itself one, it is none the less a heterogeneous multiplicity;[1] according to

[1] Bergson's fundamental objection to the theory of ideas is that it involves the assumption that, though the Idea is inert and motionless, it contains more than the moving. To introduce motion, therefore, something negative, a non-being, is required, and this degrades the Idea into all its appearances, multiplies it in space and in time. This objection, which may, as we shall see, be urged with equal force against the *élan vital*, is based on a traditional but none the less erroneous conception of the Platonic Idea. The error derives partly from the mythological manner and poetic vagaries of Plato, partly from Plato's natural tendency (in which Bergson participates) toward hypostasis, so that he often seems to deal with Ideas as if they were supersensible and inert essences, the models for all existences in space. But nobody who counts with the great critical dialogues, the

Spinoza, through the diversification of substance, because of the mind's need of conception, into infinite attributes and modes, which bear the same relation to the *free, self-caused*, and self-determining substance as the expe-

Parmenides and the *Thaeatetus*, so skeptical and negative in their outcome, can persist in the notion that the hypostasis is Plato's real intention. These dialogues, as Campbell and Jackson have clearly demonstrated, came in the middle of Plato's career, between the greater Socratic dialogues, notably the *Republic*, and the later Platonic ones, the *Philebus*, the *Timaeus*, the *Critias*, the *Laws*. The doctrine of Ideas in the *Republic* is distinguished by the elaborate mythologic form in which it is set forth; but the *Republic* is fairly rigorous beside the *Timaeus*. It is hardly likely that Plato recanted and then recanted his recantation between the writing of the *Republic* and the writing of the *Timaeus*. There can scarcely have been any contradiction, in Plato's own mind, between the theory set forth in the *Parmenides* and that in the other dialogues. If now we take those to be poetic expressions of the theory in the *Parmenides*, what is the nature of the Ideas?

To begin with, the Ideas are dynamic forces, a congeries of possible being, having actual existence and leading matter on, shaping it, organizing it. They appear most clearly in *action*. In the tenth book of the *Republic*, Plato tells us that it is the *user* of the flute who knows the real flute. "The flute-player will tell the flute-maker which of his flutes is satisfactory to the performer; he will tell him how he ought to make them, and the other will attend to his instruction." Generically, "the excellence or beauty or truth of every structure, animate or inanimate, and of every action of man, is relative to the use for which nature or the artist has intended them." This use or function is the idea, one, indivisible, simple, the definitive form of every material organization that expresses it or brings it about.

In the second place, its activity, taken in and by itself, is of the durational sort, and is truly creative. In terms of the myth

rience of the daily life bears to the *élan vital*. Substance, Nature, God, is the same interpenetration of diversities, the same uncompelled *spontaneous activity, natura naturans*. It is an *effect* which is its own *cause;* the self-

of the *Timaeus*, the goodness of God overflows spontaneously, without requiring the shock of non-being or space (μὴ ὄν). The latter does not degrade the Idea from its "eternity." Its rôle is identical with that of space in Bergson's system: it individuates and multiplies. It gives rise to Time—"the moving image of eternity"—as a spatialized version of the non-spatial activity. But, although appearing in this spatiotemporal multiplicity, the Idea, as the *Parmenides* points out, cannot itself be resident in nor divided among the things whose function it is, since, if it were, it could have neither unity nor functional character, i.e., it could not be Idea. Hence it could be neither the bond between two similars, such as the eye of the Pecten mollusk and the eye of the vertebrate, nor that unity which illuminates and accounts for the variety of the particulars. It is not a concept—i.e., a static form— yet it is what the mind knows in arresting particulars, since otherwise the knowledge of it would be irrelevant to these particulars.

Such then is the Idea, considered rigorously and not poetically. So considered, its resemblance to the *élan* in nature and in its relations to matter is extraordinarily striking. We may note, before comparing the two in detail, that in this form the Idea is not finalistic. It is a *function*, but it is a function that serves nothing external to itself. That it is not mechanical need not be argued. So that in its divergence from mechanism, its resemblance to, but non-identity with, finalism, it has one of the essential traits of the *élan*. But consider the other traits of the *élan* as Bergson exhibits it in its relations to particulars of existence, i.e., the *élan* as the function of seeing in relation to the molluscular and the vertebrate eye.

identity of the different; the simultaneity of the successive; the oneness of the many. It is the force of self-preservation of a God who loves himself with an infinite love. *Natura naturata*, thought, extension, things, are the

Since, argues M. Bergson, the Pecten and the vertebrate separate from the parent stem and grow in divergent directions long before the eye makes its appearance, every attempt to account for their identical appearance, by mechanism, finalism, neo-Darwinism, mutationism, neo-Lamarckism, invites monstrous assumptions of practically impossible coincidences of infinite complexity. The quality of the light to which all eyes respond is not as a physical cause a sufficient explanation of their organic structure. The eye is more than a physical effect. It solves a problem. It is a photograph which has been turned into a photographic apparatus. The eye makes use of light. Hence, the causal relationship between light and the eye is that between something which unwinds and releases, and that which is unwound and released. Now the latter is an *internal activity*, "something quite different from what we call an effort, for never has an effort been known to produce the slightest complication of an organ, and yet an enormous number of complications, all admirably co-ordinated, have been necessary to pass from the pigment-spot of the Infusorian to the eye of the vertebrate. . . . . Yet this, like hereditary change in a definite direction, which continues to accumulate and add to itself so as to build up a more and more complex machine, must certainly be related to some sort of effort, but to an effort of far greater depth than the individual effort, far more independent of circumstances, an effort common to most representatives of the same species, inherent in the germs they bear rather than in their substance alone, an effort thereby assured of being passed on to their descendants.

"The *élan*, then, is dynamic, transcends the individuals, yet belongs to all of them. Each of the individuals that participate in it is infinitely complex. It alone is simple. There is a con-

same mechanical necessities, the same "spatialized sequences," as the daily life. Even the freedom of man has the undetermined, self-contained quality of totality which is the central trait of the Bergsonian notion of freedom.

trast between the infinite complexity of the organ and the extreme simplicity of the function. . . . . The simplicity belongs to the object itself, and the infinite complexity to the views we take in turning round it, to the symbols by which our senses or intellects represent it to us or, more generally, to elements of a *different order*, with which we try to imitate it artificially, but with which it remains incommensurable, being of a different nature." This is almost the very language of Plato. The analogy is, however, profounder still. This different order is materiality. It does not represent means employed but obstacles avoided. "It is a negation rather than a positive reality." By right, the function of vision should reveal an infinity of things we do not see. It is enchanneled, and the eye represents the channel through which it acts. Its structure conforms to the form of the act, at once expressing and restricting it. The greater the expression, the less the restriction, consequently the difference between the pigment-spot and the vertebrate eye. Both are equally co-ordinated because they are constructed to express the same function, but the function is freest in the vertebrate. Now, how is this function in its relation to the material that it organizes different from the Platonic Idea? It isn't. It bears, as a *special* function, even the same relation to "the original impetus of life" as a particular Idea bears to the Idea of the Good. It is effected in virtue of that impetus. *It is implied therein*, implied because life, like the idea, "is more than anything else a tendency to act on inert matter."

The conclusion is, then, that the Idea resembles the *élan* in that it is a unitary force, or dynamic function, acting on inert matter, organizing it, getting itself diversely expressed through these organizations, without being itself divided or divisible.

There are, of course, the Spinozistic parallelism and eternalism, which at first blush seem antipodal to Bergsonian philosophy. But the antipodation is verbal and not real. The distinctions are conceptual,[1] and the eternalism is the maximal fulness of duration.[2] In point of fact, each mode of substance or individual entity is the interpenetration of the residuum of being, and is a mode or particular only when its substantial cause is considered as *external* to it, i.e., when, in the Bergsonian sense, it is spatialized. Conceive it in its fulness, as interpenetrated by the rest, and it is substance itself, eternal in the sense of *perduring* through all its externalizations, just as the Bergsonian *real duration* perdures through all its spatializations. Now, even as Spinoza's distinctions between appearance and reality follow from his conception of substance, so do Bergson's from his. The critics of this great and profound thinker have accused him without reason of inconsistency. His premise may be false, but

[1] Cf. *Ethica*, Book I, Definitions.

[2] Cf. Bergson, *Introduction à la métaphysique*.

his deductions are not inconsistent. If reality is what Bergson thinks it, appearance must be as he describes it. But *is* reality as he thinks it ?

II

M. Bergson has a number of striking phrases by which he designates reality. It is real or pure duration (*durée réelle*), it is a formidable thrust (*poussée formidable*), it is the onrush of life (*élan vital*), it is the innermost spirit, it is activity, it is change, it is that of which the flow gives rise to all in experience that lives and changes. But it is not, as it appears in experience, truly itself. It there appears deflected and distorted by an alien and secondary stuff with which it mixes, and which in turn it distorts. This alien or secondary stuff is matter or space, and duration must be extricated from its entanglement before it can be perceived in and by itself. This extrication is what has been accomplished in intuition. Now, what is the reality so attained to be *known as* ?

To be concrete, consider the paragraph or the page I have just written. It belongs to the common data of the daily life. It is an appearance of reality—a collection of marks and symbols, themselves spatial forms, spread over the space of the page, and standing for and representing something to which they are somehow allied and which has been the effective cause of this particular spatial complex. This something is the *one* thought which the paragraph expresses, and which you apprehend when you read the signs that compose it. But these signs are not one. The paragraph can be subdivided into sentences, each before and after another, the sentences into words, the words into letters, the letters into smaller shapes or simpler sounds, and so on endlessly. But now the idea which has so spread and ramified by means of symbols and space is not at all a thing in which I feel a definite, exclusive before-and-after, a diversity of distinct symbols with distinct meanings, having distinct relations to each other. All I feel is *one* meaning. Its *quale* is a definite tendency to write. And as I write, I am not aware of each word before I write it. I do not know what it *will be.* I discover what has become a particular word by the act of writing. The act seems to deposit the word as it moves along, and with each word deposited it has externalized itself more and more in space. It seems like the unrolling of something rolled up, but not the unrolling of a reel, on which one thing is laid *over* the other, but rather the unrolling of a thing all of whose parts are one inside the other, such that, without space, you cannot distinguish part from part, all are so absolutely one. When I read the paragraph over, I recover this unity, but not in its fulness or adequacy. I have to *recompose* it, and I feel it as a thing attained piecemeal, not at one indivisible view. Why? Because the act has been spatialized.

Suppose, now, we reverse the process, and try to roll up this act which has unrolled itself here, aiming to recover its central, indivisible tension. The mind moves hereupon not from within outward, but from without inward. Read the paragraph over several times. At the first reading, each word, perhaps each letter, stands out in its place, alone, independent, with no clear or intimate relation to the others. At the second, they all seem closer together, the space they cover seems not so great, we say the reading is swifter, we take in a sentence at a time, now, instead of a word at a time. At the third reading, this is still more true. We feel as if we were *skipping* passages, but we know that we are not, because we know that in the end we can reproduce the identical one idea which the paragraph conveys, with all its ramifications and differences, without feeling anything more than the presence of this continuous, unvarying ideational impulse. What has happened? The idea has been changed back from a fact into an act, from something *done* into something *doing*. In the repeated readings we have despatialized it. Letters, words, sentences have, in the mind, become more and more intimate. Instead of empty spaces between them they have touched, then from touching they have passed into one another, until each has become indiscernible from all and all from each. They have reverted to the status of that pure inward impulse of which they were the spatial expression, the material incarnation.

Consider, however, that this impulse, which incarnated itself in the paragraph, is but one of a countless multitude of impulses which move us. Simple as it is beside the words and sentences that express it, it must be, taken in and by itself, related to the whole of our lives as words and sentences are related to it. It must be a mere spatialization of a totality which in itself is not spatial, and which, beside it, is one and infinitely complex. Let us, then, withdraw the mind's eye from the details of life in their isolation. Let us bring them together, as we brought together the letters and sentences of our paragraph. They touch, they interpenetrate, they fuse. We behold the fulness of our selfhood, an enduring tension, which ramifies, according to need, into memories, emotions, wishes, ideas, into those mental forms which the psychologist studies singly, but which is in itself all these at one and the same time.

Nor is it alone this indivisible multiplicity. It swells, changes, grows. We feel this swelling, changing, growing within its very heart—an increase without enlargement. How else, and where else, if we abstract space absolutely? For then there is, as there must be, the actual succession of an inner experience, but such succession cannot make a distinction of before and after. A distinction would mean a juxtaposition, however slight, and juxtaposition, involving the mutual externality of the juxtaposed, is spatial. But by hypothesis and by act we have abstracted from space. We confront the innermost essence of mind in its purity. We see that it is labile, that it is pulsation, and that each pulsation, as it adds itself to its predecessors, preserves itself without distinguishing itself from them. The innermost life is a solidarity, at once self-identical and changing, "a continuous melody . . . . which carries itself on, indivisible from the beginning to the end of our conscious existence."

Now, being innermost, this life cannot help being psychical, but its psyche is not the psyche of consciousness and personality. It is the more primordial spirit of which the consciousness we know is a spatialization, a segmentation, of which the personality we are aware of is a contraction and restriction. That it is soonest and most readily to be discovered in the profundities of our own spirit is our grace, which makes humanity perhaps more its kin than any other living or moving being, since in man the cosmic spirit has most nearly liberated itself from the trammels of matter. But, in point of fact, man is a very limited concretion of it. Intuition reveals spirit as the force and go of all that moves and acts. It, and it alone, is the true metaphysical reality.

What, now, are its metaphysical characteristics?

To begin with, it is flux. It is movement and change, and these, as such, are absolutely *indivisible*. To *arrest* either is to destroy it, for it is a transition, not a condition, and can, therefore, never coincide with immobility. It may be imperceptibly brief, it may be long beyond perception, infinitely long. But it cannot be decomposed. Motion is motion and must always be that. To spatialize it is to think it in terms of its opposite, of immobility. To spatialize it is to *contradict its nature*, destroy its *identity*. That identity may be, it will be seen, a "self-contradictory" identity, but, once captured and defined, it must remain unchanged, by the *rules of the logic of identity*, throughout the discussion. To these rules Bergson rigorously adheres, in all his books. Consequently the life of all existence becomes conceived qualitatively as *one*, and its diversity and immobility become mere appearances. "There are," he writes,[1] "changes, but there are no things that change. Change has no need of a support. There are movements, but there are not necessarily invariable things that move; movement does not imply a something that possesses it" (mobile). Immobility is really appearance which the sense of sight deceives us into taking for reality. But science assures us that all matter consists in fact of movement; and a thing's movement is but a movement of movements. *H*ence, movement, and not

[1] *Perception du changement*, p. 24.

matter, is *substance*, and because of the continuity and unity of movement, the world it expresses itself by is maximally substantial and durable. "For if change is real and even constitutive of all reality, *we must think* of the past as persisting unchanged in its entirety in the one indivisible act of change,"[1] just as the notes of a melody persist unchanged in the one indivisible melody, or the meanings of the beginnings of our paragraph in the one indivisible meaning of the paragraph. Both are change and immutability at once.

Not to believe this is to be illogical, to be subject to a mere philosophical illusion. This is the illusion that real time is decomposable into instants. Such instants are fundamental in mathematics, but mathematics is only a science of space. It required that any two of them cannot be separated by a time-interval, for time is nothing more than their juxtaposition. But if they are separated by *nothing*, they are *one* and not two. Two mathematical

---

[1] The italics are mine. There is the significant deductive transition in the phrase "we must think," for the necessity is logical only.

points that touch are confounded one in the other: they interpenetrate and become an identity. Logic, hence, compels the assumption of an "interval of duration." How great this interval shall be is determined only by our capacity for attention. Let the attention expand indefinitely, and it embraces more and more and more of the past. The present, indeed, is merely the field of instant attention. To say that any portion of it is destroyed when it drops from attention would be obviously wrong. It does not cease to exist, but it becomes *past.* The past is that part of the present which the mind *neglects;* when the mind again attends to it, it becomes present. But this present is not a mere simultaneity. It is "something continually present and continually moving," "an enduring present," in which the past stays subconscious, waiting only on our needs to bring up to consciousness its appropriate part, and surging up in its totality whenever the attention on externals is relaxed, as in the cases of drowning and other forms of *vital crisis* and sudden death. Then the attention turns inward, and one's whole life unrolls before the mind's eye. Logic and experience both thus compel us to believe the past conserves itself automatically, that this self-conservation in the present is cosmic, and that it is nothing else than the indivisibility of change.

But if this is the nature of the cosmos, then, though an infinite deal is continually adding itself to whatever exists, nothing is ever, nor can be, subtracted. The substantiality and durability of the world *are* maximal. Change itself is that hidden substance which philosophers have sought, which flows through the fingers that seek by grasping to arrest it. *P*erceived in its nakedness, it is neither unstable nor immutable, but the very stuff of duration, at once indivisible and changing. Yet further: that which is *indivisibly* dynamic cannot truly be *differentiated* into cause and effect. Life is a concrete duration, the unity of the past with the present. *H*ence, if it changes, the source of the change is in itself, not in anything external. Cause is *self-caused;* effect is self-effectuation; change is creative growth, determined neither mechanically nor teleologically. In other words, life, as perceived in intuition is *free*. For, if it were not, the indivisibility of change would be destroyed, duration would be spatialized, it would be possible to forecast events infallibly. Indeed, determinism is equivalent to the possibility. Yet how is any foretelling whatever possible? *Does* not the understanding of the true nature of a cause require also the perception of its *effect?* And how is the effect to be perceived unless it is already present, and, if it is already present, what can be meant by prediction? Actually, in the inwardness of duration, not even action itself can predict. There are multitudes in the realization of an ideal that the ideal has no inkling of. Life, then, eludes prediction. But does it also escape causation? *Determinism* is not alone the possibility of prediction, it is also mechanistic causal necessity. Can life elude this necessity? Yes, however cause be defined, life can. For intuition shows us life' as persistent variation; hence, cause, defined as *unvarying* antecedent of its effect, cannot apply to life. Or take cause as common-sense tends to take it; as a compromise between the *identity* of cause and effect with time, or differentiating creative activity. Its necessity is reached by the element of identity, by the repetition of *the same*—the same number, the same quality, the same relation—in the effect. Then, as cause approaches necessity, it goes farther and farther from true activity, farther and farther from *duration* and *freedom*, where alone true causation exists. There necessity is a pure negation. There the future exists in the present only as a vague possibility. The transition from present to future is seen by intuition to be, first of all, an effort, and, secondly, an effort which does not always realize the felt possibility, yet which rests quite complete in whatever future it has brought about. Life is free.

In sum: Ultimate reality is of the same stuff as our inner life, something akin to the will, the *go* of our own existence, which "unwinds" itself—an enduring act, continuous, indivisible, substantial, creative, free, an act which is the unity and interpenetration of all that lives and moves and has its being, an incessant life which is the concretion of all durations, of all that *apparent* diversity of beings whose existence is materialization of this same formidable impetus, this *élan* of life, which is their unshatterable and persistent substance.

Such, then, is the fundamental reality which intuition reveals. How different in character and direction from the reality of the daily life, with its numerous individuals, its unchanging solids, its immutable concepts, its many checks and defeats, its few successes! How could so perfect a thing as the *élan vital* give rise to so imperfect a thing as conscious experience? Never, of itself. The ordinary world of men and things is a degradation of the *élan*. It is the disruption of its unity by means of the shock of space and matter. These are the enemy, these are the evil principle, and of the war of these with the life-force worlds are born.

What are they? *H*ow are they known? The more fundamental one is *space*. This

Bergson assumes, but whether as the meta-physical peer of *pure duration*, or something secondary and inferior, one may not absolutely say. In his earlier thinking, the notion appears that space is a Kantian form of intuition and has no reality apart from the mind that thinks it. "We have assumed," he writes in *Données immédiates de la conscience*, "the existence of a homogeneous space, and, with Kant, dis-tinguished this space from the matter that fills it. With him we have admitted that homo-geneous space is a form of our sensibility." It is an "infinitely fine network which we stretch beneath material continuity in order to make ourselves masters of it, to decompose it accord-ing to the plan of our activities and need." And this notion occurs again and again, though less explicitly stated, in his later work. Space, in *Matter and Memory*, is called a "diagram-matic design of our eventual action on matter." And in *Creative Evolution* it is more than once designated as the practical form of our intelli-gent action on things. From this point of view, it is not a secondary thing but a tertiary one, arising after a creature having need of it has been created by the evolutionary action of duration. But this view of space is incidental to the exigencies of exposition. It is not compelled by the demands of Bergson's first indefinable, *pure duration.* That requires over against it, if it is to be a factor in accounting for the course and character of experience, something with which it may combine, on which it may act. This something need not be so real as pure duration is, it may be metaphysically secondary, an inversion, but it must be opposite.

Such an opposite is space. "There is a real space without duration . . . . and a real duration, the heterogeneous moments of which interpenetrate." Space is the inversion of duration. *D*uration is interpenetration, the psychical organization of heterogeneous qualities that are immanently successive, one to another. Space is juxtaposition, the simultaneous externality of homogeneous points, whose essential character is quantitative, not qualitative. Space is an empty and homogeneous medium which is self-sufficient, void of every quality, amorphous, inert, but a "reality as solid as sensations themselves," though of a different order. Consequently space is a thing outside ourselves, "a mutual externality without succession," but an absolute reality on which we act (and it must be real therefore, since it is impossible for action to move in the unreal) and which we can and do know in its absoluteness by means of mathematics.

But mathematics, absolute, real—are not these contradictory terms? They would be, if they were not discoverable in the same intuition that reveals real duration. The only difference is that the *direction* of the intuition must be changed. Consider again the intuition of any paragraph of this chapter. Its psychic purity is attained by the incessant accumulation and interpenetration of its details. What dilutes this purity? The fact that in expression these details, instead of staying an ever-changing, fluid, tensive unity, become *external* to one another. This externalization

is *dissipation.*[1] Instead of there being from
moment to moment *more* than there was
before, there is from moment to moment less.
The force spreads, dissipates, tends to cease.
If it could cease utterly and absolutely, it
would be indistinguishable from space. That,
however, does not happen. The written or
spoken paragraph is not pure space. It is
matter. Matter is disintegrating spirit, spirit
running down, on the way to space.[2] Spirit
absolutely run down would have become its
opposite, space. Space gathered up, interpenetrated, might possibly be spirit. Consequently, behind these two "absolutes," "duration" and "space," which are inversions of one
another, opposite orders, interfering with one
another in such a way that the absence of one
means the presence of its opposite, there is a
unity "vaster and higher" of which these are
perhaps complementary differentiations, as instinct and intelligence are of the life of man.

[1] Cf. *Creative Evolution*, pp. 249–59.

[2] M. Bergson regards the second law of thermodynamics as
the most metaphysical of all physical laws.

And between these two poles of the utterly transcendent and barely suggested unity of which they are differentiations lies matter, just as real as they, to be known immediately and directly by the same intuitive act, only reversed in its duration. For matter is life "undoing itself," an absolute reality which physics studies and reveals, a thing no more than "pure duration ballasted by geometry" and partaking of the nature of both. But the intuitive act reversed in its direction is intelligence, conceptualization, analysis. The ultimate province of the intellect, consequently, must be pure space; and its ultimate form, geometry. Now intermediate between the intuition of life and the intuition of space lies the intuition of matter. This is attained in "pure perception" and in the mutually external categories and forms of the understanding, in concepts, these being static, isolated, cinematographic snapshots of the flux, catching its externalizations. "In reality, life is a movement, materiality is the inverse movement, and each of these two movements is simple, the matter which forms a world being an undivided flux, and undivided also the life that runs through it, cutting out in it living beings all along its track."[1]

*H*ence, matter, in so far as it implies duration, is also a continuum and conterminous with spirit. It involves a *before* and *after*, because it is spatial, but it involves also the linking together of these successive moments of time "by a thread of variable quality which cannot be without some likeness to the continuity of our own consciousness."　Matter endures and is, *qua* enduring, the pure flux of dynamic energy which the physicist has made the goal of his researches.　But if matter is a continuous flux of energy, it cannot be the collection of the discrete objects of experience to which we formally apply the term.　These are tertiary in that they are derivatives of matter.　They are the appearance of appearance, and are appearance to appearance.　They are the latest events in the cosmic drama whose climax is Man.

The title of this drama is Creative Evolution. Its great protagonists, its hero and villain,

[1] *Creative Evolution*, p. 249.

when M. Bergson raises the curtain for us, are *P*ure *D*uration and Space, Spirit and Matter, *Élan Vital*, and Inertia, these complementary and inverse aspects of reality, so essentially like Spinoza's *Cogitatio* and *Extensio*, attributes of *one* substance and in it, identical; so essentially like *P*lato's *idea* and non-being, absorbable in the neo-*P*latonic One. The drama arises out of the inward incompatibility of these two with one another. They cannot live together in democratic amity. The existence of the one involves the mutilation if not the destruction of the other, without concession, without compromise, even in that apparent compromise we call matter. The life-force, which is consciousness, "need to create," free, spiritual, self-cumulative, is suppressed and constrained by the rigidity and vacuity of space. A power, finite and given once for all, but containing within itself numberless potentialities, not unlike *P*latonic ideas, it cannot freely generate, fulfil, and gather within itself the *more* that continuously grows from it. For the life-force is a thing that grows by what it feeds on, and it feeds upon itself. Matter hinders and interrupts this creative growth, and hence it becomes the task of the life-force to overcome the checks and hindrances of its opponent, and to convert it from an opponent into a servant. Life succeeds in doing so, but not without a price. It pays for its conquest with its unity. In its contact with matter, life is comparable to an impulsion or an impetus; regarded in itself, it is "an immensity of potentiality, a mutual encroachment of thousands and thousands of tendencies," which nevertheless are thousands and thousands "only when regarded as outside each other, i.e., when spatialized."[1] It is compelled to divide, to adopt divergent lines of growth, in unforeseeable directions; it is compelled to "insinuate" itself into matter, "to adopt its rhythm" and movement. By so doing, however, it attains its ends. It conquers matter, and, by organizing, diverts it from its own rigidity to the uses of life. The core of this diversion is the accumulation and expenditure of stores of energy "by means of

[1] *Creative Evolution*, p. 258.

a matter as supple as possible in directions variable and unforeseen."

The first act in the conquest of matter, hence, is the evolution of the vegetable. Whatever life may feed on, its ultimate food is vegetation. "Vegetables alone gather in the solar energy and animals do but borrow it from them." By means of the "chlorophyllian function," vegetation uses the solar energy to fix the carbon of carbon-dioxid gas, and thereby to store it, for use as need be. But the vegetable is torpid, it is nearer in its action to matter than to the unexpected freedom of life. It could not both gradually store and suddenly use energy. In the vegetable, therefore, the struggle between life and matter is something of a draw. Life has gathered up matter, but the matter holds back life. Life has still not come to its own freedom.

The second act consists of the divergence of organization under the stress of this tendency toward action in variable and unforeseen directions. *Plants* went on doing as they always did, but side by side with them there developed the animal, whose characteristic it is to set free stored-up energy. This act involved many scenes, many more divergences, in not all of which did life conquer matter.

> We must take into account retrogressions, arrests, accidents of every kind. And we must remember above all that each species behaves as if the general movement of life had stopped at it, instead of passing through it. It thinks only of itself, it lives only for itself. Hence the numberless struggles that we behold in nature. Hence a discord, striking and terrible, but for which the original principle of life must not be held responsible.[1]

Alone to the compulsion of matter does the responsibility belong. For life itself is not thinkable either as pure unity or pure multiplicity. It is One that rejects the category of oneness; many, yet rejecting the category of manyness. It might have been, and would more easily have been, just itself, rather than the diversity of individuals and of societies where struggle for life is that discord "so striking and terrible." But unity and multiplicity as such belong to matter, and matter compels it to choose one of the two. Yet its choice will

[1] *Op. cit.*, pp. 254–55.

never be definitive; it will leap from one to the other indefinitely.

The pure animal, though more explosive and unaccountable than the plant, is automatic. Its explosions are marked by the absence of variety, by sameness. Spirit is not yet completely liberated. To become so, it needs an organized matter of maximum instability. The making and maintenance of this is the third act of life's struggle with matter, the climactic act, in which it asserts itself, master of matter at last, by means of the human brain. This differs from other brains in that "the number of mechanisms it can set up, and consequently the choice that it gives as to which among them shall be released, is unlimited." This makes it differ from other brains not in degree, but in kind.[1] So "with man, consciousness breaks the chain. In man and man alone it sets itself free."[2] His body is his machine which he uses as he pleases. Because of his complex brain with its capacity for

[1] *Ibid.*, p. 263.
[2] *Ibid.*, p. 264.

opposed motor mechanisms; because of his language with its capacity for incarnating consciousness in an immaterial body; because of his social life with its capacity for storing and preserving effort as language preserves thought, man is free. In him Spirit triumphs completely over Matter, *D*uration over Space, the Life-Force over Inertia. The drama has a happy ending. Seeing the world so,

we feel ourselves no longer isolated in humanity, humanity no longer seems isolated in the nature that it dominates. As the smallest grain of dust is bound up with our entire solar system, drawn along with it in that undivided movement of descent which is materiality itself, so all organized beings, from the humblest to the highest, from the first origins of life to the time in which we are, and in all places as in all times, do but evidence a single impulsion, the inverse of the movement of matter, and in itself indivisible. All the living hold together, and all yield to the same tremendous push. The animal takes its stand on the plant, man bestrides animality, and the whole of humanity, in space and time, is one immense army galloping beside and before and behind each of us in an overwhelming charge able to beat down every resistance and clear the most formidable obstacles, perhaps even death.[1]

[1] *Op. cit.*, pp. 270-71.

III

There exists in philosophy, writes William James,[1] a plain alternative. Is the manyness in oneness that indubitably characterizes the world we inhabit, a property only of the absolute whole of things, so that you must postulate that one-enormous-whole indivisibly as the *prius* of there being any many at all—in others words, start with the rationalistic block-universe, entire, unmitigated, complete?—or can the finite elements have their own aboriginal forms of manyness in oneness, and where they have no immediate oneness still be continued into one another by intermediary terms—each one of these terms being one with its next neighbors, and yet the total "oneness" never getting absolutely complete?

Of this alternative, Bergson, we have seen, chooses explicitly neither horn. In its intrinsic nature pure duration is an ineffable *totum simul*, not yet differentiated into the inverse movements of life and matter, and rejecting, like Plotinos' One, the categories of both *oneness* and *manyness*. Implicitly Bergson chooses the former of these alternatives. He observes with James that experience has contradictory

[1] *A Pluralistic Universe*, p. 326.

aspects, that it possesses both oneness and manyness at the same time. Their co-presence in experience gives rise to innumerable philosophic difficulties, notably the great antinomies which troubled philosophers from Zeno to Kant. How surmount the difficulties, how solve the antinomies? If you study their basis and origin, you observe that they arise from the attempt to explain manyness by oneness and oneness by manyness. *Philosophic salvation*, then, must lie in a new principle of explanation. What shall it be, and be new? Why, simply rendering unto Caesar that which is Caesar's and unto God that which is God's. No wonder logical puzzles and essential contradictions persist in philosophy. They must, since they are no more than attempts to reconcile the irreconcilable. Segregate these, let the same account for the same alone, let each principle account only for itself, and the puzzle disappears. You find, to begin with, the absolute oneness, the undesignable and transcendent unity of life, accounting for motion, action, continuity, for all that has the quality

of unity. In the Bergsonian world, the qualitative basis is given *at once*, and whatever
comings there are, are somewhat forecast in the
"original impetus" and contingent on its
material obstacles: "Life does not proceed by
the association and addition of elements, but
by the dissociation and division." It is creation that goes on forever in virtue of an initial
movement, which constitutes the unity of the
organic world. It is the continuity of a "single
and identical *élan*" which has split up along
the lines of a divergent evolution. It is what
is "common" to all divergences, and these are
complements one of the other, in such wise
that their very complementariness and harmony
contain and presuppose and depend on an
"identity of impulsion." The quoted terms
are Bergson's own. On the other hand, you
find the absolute manyness, the Bradleyan
unrelatable discreteness which is the designable
diversity of space, accounting for all that
derives from it. And so long as you confine
each principle to its own sphere, you get into
no difficulties. Seek, however, to take the

concrete individuality of experience at its
face value, as *manyness-in-oneness*, and try to
explain one by the other—then, presto, all the
difficulties reappear. Time, action, life, can
explain only those things which are identical
with them; space, inertness, matter, can explain
only those things which are identical with them.
Antinomies arise when the explanations offered
are transverse. In point of fact they are not
alternatives; each member of the pair is valid
in its own field. If, therefore, the universe seems
disorderly, it *seems* so merely. There is no real
disorder. There is only the substitution of
the spatial for the temporal order, the material
for the spiritual, and conversely. Chaos and
the void are pseudo-ideas. The realities are
spirit and space. Ultimately, of course, these
two fields may be derivable from something
vaster and higher, a unity which embraces and
reconciles both. *H*ow, is not written. The
course of experience is nevertheless to be ex-
plained by these diverse and opposite principles.

*H*ence, unity immediately and ultimately
includes for Bergson a one-enormous-whole

indivisibly given as the *prius* of the vital or organic many. Diversity, similarly, involves an absolutely irreconcilable externality. Both of these are *transcendental* principles and not discoverable as such in the immediacies of experience. Each requires, in order to be perceived, the absoluteness of intuition, the intuition of the spirit, in the one case; of the intellect, in the other. Each is the limit reached by a rigorous application of the identity logic. Consequently the Bergsonian philosophy is involved in both the fallacies of traditional metaphysics —the fallacy of division which is the differentia of apriorism and the fallacy of composition which is the differentia of empiricism. Each of these fallacies is a metaphysical dogma. One says that the part has no reality save in terms of the whole; the other says that the whole is nothing more than an aggregate of parts. What is significant is the bond that unites the two and makes them harmonious parts of one identical tradition. This bond is the dogma of *unreality of relations*. For apriorism, relations have ever been internal, so that the universe was always a block: the whole concentrated in every point. For empiricism relations have been utterly external such that the entities or impressions which compose the flux of experience could never touch, never influence each other, never make any real difference to each other. This double status of relations is accepted *in toto* by Bergson. In the *élan*, the interpenetration of the heterogeneous is such that distinctions cannot be made and hence must be artificially supplied by the mind; in space the discreteness is so absolute that nothing happens there unless a mind internalizes its contents.[1]

Now, if any one thing more than any other sets James beyond the philosophic tradition and distinguishes radical and immediate empiricism from both the empiricism and the apriorism of tradition, it is his readiness to take relations, conjunctive as well as disjunctive, internal no less than external, at their face value, whenever and wherever they appear. Neither the substantial flux, he points out, interpenetrative to

[1] Cf. *Creative Evolution*, pp. 147–49, 250, 356, 367–68.

the uttermost, nor yet the discrete space, external to the uttermost, is barren of *conjunctive* relations. Neither one is oppugnant to and completely exclusive of the other. There is not a block of oneness that we call life, and a hegemony of bare homogeneous manyness that we call space, nor yet an ineffable *totum simul* which is, and still is *not* that, like Plotinos' One, rejecting both categories. There is a *real* combination of manyness and oneness in which the relations that bind, and whose action makes the oneness, are as immediate data of sense-perception as the terms that are bound; and the relations that distinguish, and whose actions make the manyness, have as legitimate a metaphysical status as the terms that they differentiate. There is no *whole* in which all that is to be is somehow foreshadowed and predetermined; there is no contingency which is extra-spiritual and involves no difference in the quality of spirit. There is no necessary conservation of the past. *Destruction* is as real as creation, contingency is a trait of every entity that exists, and, what exists, exists piecemeal, and not in terms of a whole, indivisible act which cuts through matter.

The divergence here indicated is so profound that it seems strange that any similarity whatever should exist between these two thinkers, and stranger still that the one should feel himself indebted to the other for anything whatever. But does not, indeed, the existence of such a conjunction amid such diversity constitute a prima facie exhibition of the manyness-and-oneness of experience which James points out? We have seen[1] that both these thinkers are, from the outset, temporalists, that both are agreed as to the inadequacy of static concepts to act as substitutes for activities, and as to the distortion of reality which arises when concepts are taken as the identical equivalents of things which they represent. Concepts, like the rest of reality, are only self-revealing, and in use they are controllers rather than revealers. But here the resemblance stops. The self which concepts reveal is the selfhood of matter and space according to Bergson, and

[1] *Supra*, chap. ii.

the dimension in which they exist is not the dimension of life at all. They are metaphysically as well as functionally tertiary. Not so for James. Their metaphysical status is not different from that of any other entity; it is their function that is different, and it is the confusion of status with function that is, for him, the source of metaphysical error.

Now, it is with Bergson's treatment of concepts in their relation to activity, movement, and life that James is most concerned. What is it that he gains from Bergson? *He* gains, to begin with, freedom to accept experience at its face value; he gains, in the second place, confirmation that this face value is not illusory.

The assumption which underlay James's treatment of the greater problems of psychology was the assumption of the dualism of mind and matter. The assumption was methodological, not metaphysical, and the theory of psychophysical parallelism was dirempted at one point by a theory of interaction for which the warrant was empirico-ontologic, rather than a logical deduction from the parallelistic premise.

Logic demanded the correlation of brain states with mental states. But whereas brain states might be compounded, mental states could not so be. They were fluid, evanescent, not perdurable, and for each brain state there could be but one and only one mental state.

The so-called mental compounds are simple *psychic reactions of a higher type. The form itself of them . . . . . is something new.*[1] We can't say that awareness of the alphabet as such is nothing more than twenty-six awarenesses, each of a separate letter; for those are twenty-six distinct awarenesses of single letters *without* others, while their so-called sum is one awareness of every letter *with* its comrades. There is thus something new in the collective consciousness. It means the same letters, indeed, but it knows them in this novel way. It is safer . . . . to treat the consciousness of the alphabet as a twenty-seventh fact, the substitute and not sum of the twenty-six simpler consciousnesses, and to say that while under certain physiological conditions they alone are produced— other, more complex physiological conditions result in in its production instead. . . . . The higher thoughts . . . . are psychic units, not compounds; but, for all that, they may know together as a collective multitude the very same objects which under other condi-

---

[1] The italics are mine.

tions are known separately by as many simple thoughts. The theory of combination, I was forced to conclude, is thus untenable, being both logically nonsensical and practically unnecessary.[1]

Such is the logical outcome enforced by the assumption of psychophysical parallelism. But this is an outcome which, while true in many instances, flies none the less in the face of the facts in many others. In the physical world, for instance,

we make with impunity the assumption that one and the same material object can figure in an indefinitely large number of different processes at once. An air particle or an ether particle "compounds" the different directions of movement imprinted on it without obliterating their several individualities. It delivers them distinct, on the contrary, at as many several "receivers" (ear, eye, or what not) as may be "tuned" to that effect.[2]

Why, distinctly true in physics, should this not also be true in psychology? In the "experience of activity" what is "the true relation of the longer-span to the shorter-span activities"?

[1] *A Pluralistic Universe*, pp. 188–89.

[2] *Essays in Radical Empiricism*, pp. 125–26.

When, for example, a number of "ideas" . . . . grow confluent in a larger field of consciousness, do the smaller activities still coexist with the wider activities then experienced by the conscious subject? And, if so, do the wide activities accompany the narrow ones inertly or do they exert control? Or do they perhaps utterly supplant and replace them and short circuit their effects?[1]

Wundt and other psychologists had had the advantage of conceiving the "compounding of consciousness" as analogous to the compounding of matter. They exceeded thereby strict logic, and until he had read Bergson, James was unwilling to commit this excess. But the theory of consciousness which Bergson maintains and defends is, significantly enough, exactly that which, because of his reading of Bergson's works, James abandons. The idea of the alphabet is, indeed, for Bergson, a "simple psychic reaction of a higher type" of which "the form itself is something new." It is true that, according to the Bergsonian philosophy, the earlier states are conserved as memory, but not each in its individuality after

[1] *A Pluralistic Universe*, p. 394.

the analogy of physical motions cited above, but penetrated through and through by all the rest, "every letter with its comrades," and the whole heterogeneous unity related *internally*. So that the consciousness of the aphabet *is* a twenty-seventh fact, a psychic unit, not a compound, a thing absolutely new. There can be found in Bergson's notion of compounding nothing analogous to a physical compounding of entities to which James has committed himself. Extraordinary and paradoxical! until the candid reader of James observes that what concerns him in the Bergsonian philosophy is not its conceptions of spirit and of matter, but its critique of intellectualism, its analysis of the relations of concepts to motion, to the continuum, to the perceptual flux. This analysis frees James from the decrees of logic and permits him to accept unequivocally the self-portrayal of immediate experience.

And in all this Bergson is still at the position in psychology that James has abandoned, and where James strikes out toward a neutralistic pluralism and radical empiricism, Bergson erects the methodological assumptions of psychophysics into the ontological dualism of spirit and matter of the philosophic tradition, subdued by the shadow of a *P*lotinian monism.

IV

James's acceptance of the principle of compounding, in essence identical with that of naturalistic physics, completely destroyed, for him, the barrier between mind and matter, a barrier already considerably broken in the development of his philosophy of pure experience,[1] with its insistence on the experiential reality of relations, and on the metaphysical equality of all experiential entities. It is no more than the acknowledgment of the ontologic validity of the manyness-and-oneness which is the face of experience, and its salvation from the stigma of "appearance" which tradition, and Bergson with it, tend to attach to it as such. Reality is a compenetration, but not that complete and utter internalization of qualities which Bergson calls spirit. Reality

[1] Cf. *Essays in Radical Empiricism*, Essays III and IV.

is a multiplicity, yet not that complete and utter externalization of qualityless points which Bergson calls space and the goal of matter. *H*ere and now, where things happen, in the region of all temporal reality without exception, exists this many-in-one. The oneness is the sensible continuity of the stream of experience. *H*erein every element is really *next* to its neighbors, every point of flux, a conflux, so that there is literally nothing between. The manyness are the elements which exist there, so continuous.

Nothing real is absolutely simple . . . . every smallest bit of experience is a *multum in parvo* plurally related, ... each relation is one aspect, character, or function, way of its being taken or way of its taking something else; and . . . . a bit of reality when actually engaged in one of these relations is not *by that very fact* engaged in all the other relations simultaneously. The relations are not all what the French call *solidaires* with one another. Without losing its identity a thing can either take up or drop another thing.[1]

This offers us a multitude, a multiverse, but our multiverse still makes a "universe," for every part, tho it may not be in actual or immediate

[1] *A Pluralistic Universe*, pp. 322–23.

connexion, is nevertheless in some possible or mediated connexion with every other part, however remote, through the fact that each part hangs together with its next neighbors in inextricable interfusion. The type of union, it is true, is different from the monistic type of *alleinheit*. It is not a universal co-implication or integration *durcheinander*. It is what I call the strung-along type, the type of continuity, contiguity, or concatenation.[1]

What is remarkable about this statement is the extraordinary sobriety of judgment and clearness of vision so characteristic of James and so likely to cause men of lesser restraint and narrower insight to accuse him of inconsistency. The unity and continuity here described are those of an utter and transitive nextness. They are the exact opposite of Bergson's unity and continuity which are the *solidarity* of compenetrating qualities, a literal integration *durcheinander*. It would seem as if James were logically required to pass from a somewhat similar solidarity in the bits of experience, every portion of which is somehow its own *H*egelian other, to the similar solidarity of the whole. This is exactly what, under the

[1] *A Pluralistic Universe*, p. 325.

compulsion of logic, Bergson does. But for James, such a procedure would be a fallacy of composition, and he insists on characterizing the larger units of experience as they appear, and on taking them at their face value. *H*e has committed himself to the theory of compounding which Bergson freed him to adopt, *in toto*. The parts do retain their identity and do function in the wholes which they constitute in terms of their own unique natures, and the wholes again do have powers and attributes and efficacies not given to the parts and in no sense foreshadowed in them. Each must be taken in its individual integrity and judged on its own showing. *H*ence, the *happenings*, which constitute temporal reality, are not *one* happening, unique, indivisible, concrete, substantial; they are truly plural and truly *discrete*. Inwardly complex and interpenetrative, with "rearward and forward looking ends," they are outwardly just *next* each other, and their overflowing at their edges is not through and through. The relations that bind are external as well as internal.

Consequently, while each *pulse* of experience is an interpenetrative unity of past and present, a *passing* moment, it is only *next* its fellows and not absolutely in them. Reality is genuinely discrete and grows by drops.

If a bottle had to be emptied by an infinite number of successive decrements, it is mathematically impossible that the emptying should ever positively terminate. In point of fact, however, bottles and coffee-pots empty themselves by a finite number of decrements, each of definite amount. Either a whole drop emerges or nothing emerges from the spout. If all change went thus dropwise, so to speak, *if real time sprouted or grew by units of duration of determinate amount*,[1] just as our perceptions of it grow by pulses, there would be no Zenonian paradoxes or Kantian antinomies to trouble us. All our sensible experiences, as we get them immediately, do thus change by discrete pulses of perception, each of which keeps us saying "more, more, more," or "less, less, less," as the definite increments or diminutions make themselves felt.[2]

But is not the continuity of a reality so describable "really" discontinuity? Yes, but only in logic, not in fact. The discontinuity is consonant with the "radically pluralist, empiri-

[1] The italics are mine.

[2] *Op. cit.*, p. 231; cf. above, p. 44.

cist, perceptualist position, and James adopts it in principle, qualifying it, however, so as to fit it closely to perceptual experience."[1] The principle is that reality changes "by steps finite in number and discrete." The qualification is that such changing involves not an experiential but a mathematico-logical discontinuity. "The mathematical definition of continuous quantity as 'that between any two elements or terms of which there is another term' is directly opposed to the more empirical or perceptual notion that anything is continuous when its parts appear as immediate next neighbors, with absolutely nothing between."[2] The discontinuous, thus, is also at the same time continuous. The continuity is not that which is merely thought, or deduced, or symbolized; it is the continuity discovered and perceived. *Here*, again, the principle of *compounding* forced on James by experience in the face of ratiocination is rigorously applied. His empiricism shows itself once more to be radical.

[1] *Some Problems of Philosophy*, p. 172.
[2] *Ibid.*, p. 187.

V

Such, then, is the structure of reality considered in its nearness and intimacy. Is it characterized by a prepotent order or a duality of orders? *Does* it, as a whole, contain a dominant stuff, or substance? Again, to say so would be to commit the fallacy of composition. With respect to order, experience as a whole presents itself as a chaos or quasi-chaos, i.e., a much-at-once. Its constitution appears to be, at least, non-rational, and there is to be found

no good warrant for ever suspecting the existence of any reality of a higher denomination than that distributed and strung along and flowing sort of reality we finite beings swim in.[1] .... No more of reality collected together at once is extant anywhere perhaps, than in my experience of reading this page, or in yours of listening. .... Sensational experiences *are* their "own others" .... both internally and externally. Inwardly they are one with their parts, and outwardly they pass continuously into their next neighbors, so that events separated by years of time in a man's life hang together unbrokenly by intermediary events.[2]

[1] *A Pluralistic Universe*, p. 213.

[2] Ibid., p. 285.

We are, it would seem, only warranted in concluding that

experience as a whole is a process of time, whereby innumerable particular terms lapse and are superseded by others that follow upon them by transitions which, whether disjunctive or conjunctive in content, are themselves experiences, and must in general be accounted at least as real as the terms which they relate. . . . . The whole system . . . . as immediately given presents itself as a quasi-chaos through which one can pass out of an initial term in many directions and yet end in the same terminus, moving from next to next by a great many possible paths.[1]

Again,

there is vastly more discontinuity in the sum total of experiences than we commonly suppose. The objective nucleus of every man's experience, his own body, is, it is true, a continuous percept; and equally continuous as a percept (though we may be inattentive to it) is the material environment of that body, changing by gradual transition when the body moves. But the distant parts of the physical world are at all times absent from us, and form conceptual objects merely, into the perceptual reality of which our life inserts itself at points discrete and relatively rare. Round their several objective nuclei, partly shared and common and partly discrete, of the real physical world, innumerable thinkers, pursuing their several lines of physically true cogitation, trace paths that intersect

[1] *Essays in Radical Empiricism*, p. 134.

one another only at discontinuous perceptual points, and the rest of the time are quite incongruent; and around all the nuclei of shared "reality" . . . . floats the vast cloud of experiences that are wholly subjective, that are non-substitutional, that find not even an eventual ending for themselves in the perceptual world —the mere day-dreams and joys and sufferings and wishes of the individual minds. They exist *with* one another, indeed, and with the objective nuclei; but, out of them, it is probable that to all eternity no interrelated system of any kind will ever be made.[1]

The world is radically a pluralism, existence is piecemeal, and "piecemeal existence is independent of complete collectibility. . . . . Some facts at any rate exist only distributively, or in form of a set of eaches, which (even if in infinite number) need not in any intelligible sense either experience themselves or get experienced by anything else, as members of an All."

Metaphysical and experiential beings are, we may conclude, coincident with respect to order. There is neither monism nor dualism nor alternation of two orders. There are just terms and relations, conjunctive and disjunctive. The multiverse is discrete and radically plural. Reality is externally related.

[1] *Essays in Radical Empiricism*, pp. 65, 66.

Everything you can think of, however vast or inclusive, has . . . . a genuinely "external" environment of some sort or amount. Things are "with" one another in many ways, but nothing includes everything, or dominates over everything. The word "and" trails along after every sentence. Something always escapes. "Ever not quite" has to be said of the best attempts made anywhere in the universe at attaining all-inclusiveness. The pluralistic world is thus more like a federal republic than like an empire or a kingdom. However much may be collected, however much may report itself as present at any effective centre of consciousness or action, something is self-governed and absent and unreduced to unity.[1]

Moreover, metaphysical is coincident with experiential being not alone in its discreteness, but in its continuity. The latter is constituted by "positively conjunctive transition." This involves neither chasm nor leap.

Being the very original of what we mean by continuity, it makes a continuum wherever it appears. Our fields of experience have no more definite boundaries than have our fields of view. Both are fringed forever by a *more* that continuously develops, and that continuously supersedes them as life proceeds.[2] . . . .

Life is in the transition as much as in the terms connected; often, indeed, it seems to be there more

[1] *A Pluralistic Universe*, pp. 321, 322.
[2] *Essays in Radical Empiricism*, pp. 70, 71.

emphatically, as if our spurts and sallies forward were the real firing-line of the battle, were like the thin line of flame advancing across the dry autumnal field which the farmer proceeds to burn. In this line we live prospectively as well as retrospectively. It is "of" the past, inasmuch as it comes expressly by the past's continuation; it is "of" the future in so far as the future, when it comes, will have continued it.[1]

Reality is a mosaic in which the pieces cling together by their edges, the transitions between them forming their cement. From this mosaic no experiential entity is excluded. Particularly, time is harmoniously copresent with space, and conversely. There is no ontological alternation or substitution of one for the other as in the Bergsonian account, no difference by the presence or absence of extension.[2]

Far back as we go, the flux, both as a whole and in its parts, is that of things conjunct and separated. The great continua of time, space, and the self envelop everything betwixt them, and *flow together without interfering.*[3] The things that they envelop come as separate in some ways and as continuous in others. Some sensations coalesce with some ideas, and others

---

[1] *Essays of Radical Empiricism*, p. 87.

[2] I*bid.*, p. 31.

[3] I*bid.*, pp. 94–95. The italics are mine.

are irreconcilable. *Qualities* compenetrate one space
or exclude each other from it. . . . . In all this the
*continuities and the discontinuities are absolutely co-
ordinate matters* of immediate feeling. . . . . And the
feeling of continuance in no wise jars upon the simultaneous feeling of novelty.

In all this, again, the unity or continuity is
that of "concatenation," not of "consolida-
tion." "The world hangs together from
next to next in a variety of ways, so that when
you are off one thing you can always be onto
something else without ever dropping out of
your world."[1]

As there is no dominant and prevailing *order*
in reality, but a compenetration and a conflict
of all orders, so also there is no dominant and
prevailing *substance.* The stuff of reality is
whatever it appears to be—"*that,* just what
appears, space, intensity, flatness, heaviness,
brownness, whatnot." "There is no general
stuff of which experience at large is made.
There are as many stuffs as there are 'natures'
in the things experienced."[2] Particularly is

[1] *Some Problems of Philosophy*, p. 31.
[2] *Essays in Radical Empiricism*, pp. 26, 27.

it to be denied that there exists any such special order of dominations as mind and matter, taken metaphysically—and Bergson so takes them. "There is . . . . no aboriginal stuff or quality of being, contrasted with that of which material objects are made, out of which our thoughts of them are made."[1] There is no "impalpable inner flowing" given as an immediate consciousness of consciousness itself.[2] There is no inextension:

Descartes for the first time defined thought as the absolutely unextended, and later philosophers have accepted the description as correct. But what possible meaning has it to say that, when we think of a foot-rule or a square yard, extension is not attributable to our thought? Of every extended object, the *adequate* mental picture must have all the extension of the object itself. The difference between objective and sub-jective extension is one of relation to a context solely. In the mind the various extents maintain no necessarily stubborn order relatively to each other, while in the physical world they bound each other stably, and added together, make the real enveloping Unit which we believe in and call real Space. As "outer" they carry themselves adversely, so to speak, to one another,

[1] *Essays in Radical Empiricism*, p. 3.
[2] *Ibid.*, p. 6.

exclude one another, and maintain their distances; while as "inner" their order is loose and they form a *durcheinander* in which the unity is lost. . . . . The two worlds differ, not by the presence or absence of extension, but by the relations of the extensions which in both worlds exist.[1]

Bergson, observing the same data, identifies the relations with the substance and rules extension out of the mental world altogether. James goes by the facts. For him there is no intuition of thought "flowing as life within us, in absolute contrast with the objects which it so unremittingly escorts."[2] There is no mind-stuff, there is no matter. There are only thoughts in the concrete and there are things, and thoughts in the concrete are made of the same sort of stuff as things are. Even affectional facts, valuations, emotions, and so on indefinitely, do not belong to one realm exclusively, but are by usage determined now to this place, now to that.

If "physical" and "mental" meant two different kinds of intrinsic nature immediately, intuitively, and

[1] *Ibid.*, pp. 30, 31; cf. also *A Pluralistic Universe*, pp. 253, 254, cited in chap. ii.

[2] *Essays in Radical Empiricism*, p. 36.

infallibly discernible, and each fixed forever in whatever bit of experience it qualified, one does not see how
there could ever have arisen any room for doubt or
ambiguity. But, if, on the contrary, these words are
words of sorting, ambiguity is natural. For then, as
soon as the relations of a thing are sufficiently various,
it can be sorted variously. Take a mass of carrion,
for example, and the "disgustingness" which for us
is part of the experience. The sun caresses it, and the
zephyrs woo it as if it were a bed of roses. So the disgustingness fails to *operate* within the realm of suns
and breezes—it does not function as a physical quality.
But the carrion "turns our stomach" by what seems a
direct operation—it *does* function physically, therefore, in that limited part of physics. We can take it
as physical or as non-physical according as we take it
in the narrower or wider context, and conversely, of
course, we must treat it as non-mental or as mental.

Our body itself is the primary instance of the
ambiguous. Sometimes I treat my body purely as
a part of outer nature. Sometimes, again, I think
of it as "mine," I sort it with the "me," and then
certain local changes and determinations in it pass for
spiritual happenings. Its breathing is my "thinking,"
its sensorial adjustments are my "attention," its
kinaesthetic alterations are my "efforts," its visceral
perturbations are my "emotions." The obstinate
controversies that have arisen over such statements
as these . . . . prove how hard it is to decide by bare
introspection what it is in experiences that shall make
them either spiritual or material. It surely can be
nothing intrinsic in the individual experience. It is

their way of behaving toward each other, their system of relations, their function; and all these things vary with the context in which we find it opportune to consider them.

Empirically and radically then, "there is no original spirituality or materiality of being, intuitively discerned."[1]

Even concepts, secondary formations though they are, in substance less than, and in the functions, additive to, the experiential flux, are not of another and different metaphysical status. Their stuff is like that of the residual reality. They are the "natures" in the things experienced, and their *being* is an act that is part of the flux of feeling, while their *meanings* are part of the concrete disjunctions and discretenesses which diversify that same flux.[2] They too have the many-and-oneness which comes in every instance of experience, and are as real as percepts. *Percepts* and they "interpenetrate and melt together, impregnate and fertilize each other. Neither, taken alone,

[1] *Essays in Radical Empiricism*, pp. 148, 152–54.

[2] Cf. *Some Problems of Philosophy*, p. 48.

knows reality in its completeness. We need
them both, as we need both of our legs to walk
with."[1]   *Percepts and concepts are consubstantial.*

They are made of the same kind of stuff, and melt
into each other when we handle them together.   How
could it be otherwise when the concepts are like
evaporations out of the bosom of perception, into
which they condense again whenever practical service
summons them?   No one can tell, of the things he now
holds in his hands and reads, how much comes in
through his eyes and fingers, and how much, from his
apperceiving intellect, unites with that and makes of
it this particular "book."   The universal and the particular parts of experience are literally immersed in
each other, and both are indispensable.   Conception
is not like a painted hook, on which no real chain can
be hung; for we hang concepts upon percepts, and
percepts upon concepts, interchangeably and indefinitely. . . . . The world we practically live in is one
in which it is impossible, except by theoretic retro-
spection, to disentangle the contributions of intellect
from those of sense. . . . . Intellectual reverbera-
tions enlarge and prolong the perceptual experience
which they envelop, associating it with the remoter
parts of existence.   And the ideas of these in turn
work like those resonators that pick out partial tones

Cf. *Some Problems of Philosophy*, pp. 52, 53.

in complex sounds. They help us to decompose our percept into parts and to abstract and isolate its elements.[1]

In sum, for James, the fundamental fact is the immediate experience taken at its face value. As such it is a much-at-once, containing terms and relations, continuities and discretenesses, inextricably mingled. There exists a real compounding, so that the empirical individual data, both those that are substantive and those that are transitive, maintain their identities and yet compose larger wholes, present at the same time and in the same way: wholes which are truly wholes and exhibit new characteristics neither implied by nor otherwise foreshadowed in the aboriginal elements of which these wholes are composed. And all of these, although they must be taken temporally, are absolutely co-ordinate matters of being, there existing no one dominant order, no one dominant substance, but a congeries and aggregate of "natures" and orders, metaphysically the peers one of the other.

[1] *Ibid.*, pp. 107, 108.

VI

The divergence of this insight, which is the insight of radical empiricism (an insight which does take reality at its face value, absolutely without reservations), from the philosophic tradition, both the "empirical" and "rationalist" are patent. Patent also must be its contrast with the Bergsonian philosophy. From that, indeed, its difference extends still more deeply. It reaches out to those perceptions which both great thinkers have so vigorously defended against the enemy, and concerning the reality of which they are unanimous. Those are the perceptions of *activity*, of *freedom*, of *novelty*, of *causation*. By Bergson, these terms are practically equated one with the other, and finally identified with *élan vital* and *durée réelle*. To his thinking, they are, in a word, simply different symbols designating his fundamental metaphysical intuition—real duration, spirit, life. To James they stand for distinct experiential data, coimplicative perhaps, but not identical one with the other, and certainly not identical with a predominating metaphysical substance.

Taken in its broadest sense any apprehension of something doing, is an experience of activity. . . . . Mere, restless, zig-zag movement, or a wild *Ideen-flucht* or *Rhapsodie der Wahrnehmung*, as Kant would say, would constitute an active from an inactive world. . . . . The word "activity" has no imaginable content whatever save these experiences of process, obstruction, strivings, strain, or release, ultimate *qualia* as they are of the life given us to be known.[1]

And that is all. James denies categorically that he maintains "a metaphysical principle of activity." There is no pragmatic need nor aesthetic justification of one.[2] Now these experiences of activity, "ultimate *qualia*" as they are of life, are all experiences of activity and of nothing more; they are not all experiences of freedom and of novelty. These last words mean that what happens in the world is not pure repetition, which would still be activity, but that each fresh situation comes "with an original touch." But the "original touch" does not imply a "principle of free will," for what could it do, "except rehearse the

[1] *A Pluralistic Universe*, p. 377; *Some Problems of Philosophy*, p. 212.

[2] *A Pluralistic Universe*, p. 391, note.

phenomenon beforehand" ?[1]   It implies simply
that in some respect the future is not coimplicative with the past, that there are real and utterly
unforeseeable *disjunctive* additions with nothing
to link them "save what the words 'plus,' 'with,'
or 'and' stand for"; that, to use James's familiar metaphor, reality grows by drops; that
future and past are discrete, that activities are
plural and not one.

So James is not involved in that Eleatic-
Heracleitan admixture, which is characteristic at once of neo-*P*latonism and Bergsonian
temporalism. For to the latter the *poussée
formidable* is given all at once and once for
all, and it is an act continuous and indivisible
and substantial, of which the discrete actions of
experience, all the activities designated and
enumerated by James, are but spatial corrup-
tions and deteriorations. Creation is individuation of the unindividual, under the shock

---

[1] *A Pluralistic Universe*, p. 392.   That is really what Bergson's *durée réelle* does, since in it everything is somehow foreshadowed and prepared for, though not predetermined.   Change
is a sort of explication of the implicit or exteriorization of the
internal.

or opposition of matter. *D*uration is somewhat different from this creation, for it requires that the past shall be both altered and unaltered in an internal and through-and-through addition, which is not altogether an addition, to the "temporal extent" already given. Genuine chance is precluded from such a reality, although unforeseeability, and *freedom* in the Spinozistic sense of the word, alteration that springs out of the *total nature* of the *élan* are not. Contingency does not reside in the *élan* itself; it resides in the *matter* on which it acts. The *élan* would still have diversified in the direction of intelligence and of instinct, even though the particular natural energy of which it made use were not carbonaceous, and hence no men and no bees and no ants were formed. The capacity for them would, of course, still reside in it as a foreshadowing tension; it would simply not have been corrupted toward extension by means of carbon.

Such considerations are, however, entirely foreign to James's views of chance or contingency. For him contingency is real here and now, and *chance* is genuine immediately. In this view, activity becomes co-ordinate and equivalent with causation, as freedom and chance do with novelty. Now causation, concretely taken, involves for James, as for Bergson, something dramatic, a sustaining of a felt purpose against felt obstacles, and over-coming or being overcome. The content of "sustaining" is what it is "known-as," nothing more. It is *not* the rejection of either "final" or "efficient" causation by a *tertium quid*, but (at least in our personal activities which we most readily experience) the coalescence of both as activity. Such a coalescence is durational. Something persists. But also something is lost, and something is gained.

The activity sets up more effects than it proposes literally. The end is defined beforehand in most cases only as a general direction, along which all sorts of novelties and surprises lie in wait.[1]

The novelties and surprises are utter and complete.

[1] *Some Problems of Philosophy*, p. 213.

In every series of real terms, not only do the terms themselves and their environment change, but we change, and their *meaning* for us changes, so that new kinds of sameness and types of causation continually come into view and appeal to our interest.   Our earlier lines, having grown irrelevant, are then dropped. The old terms can no longer be substituted nor the relations "transferred," because of so many new dimensions into which experience has opened. . . . . Professor Bergson, believing as he does in a Heracleitan *devenir réel*, ought, if I rightly understand him, positively to deny that in the actual world the logical axioms hold good without qualification.   Not only, according to him, do terms change, so that after a certain time the very elements of things are no longer what they were, but relations also change, so as no longer to obtain in the same identical way between the new things that have succeeded upon the old ones.   If this were really so, then however indefinitely sames might be substituted for sames in the logical world of nothing but pure sameness, in the world of real operations every line of sameness actually started and followed up would eventually give out and cease to be traceable farther.   Sames of the same in such a world will not always (or rather, in a strict sense, will never) be the same as one another, for in such a world there *is* no literal or ideal sameness among numerical differents. Nor in such a world will it be true that the cause of the cause is unreservedly the cause of the effect, for if we follow the line of real causation, instead of contenting ourselves with Hume's and Kant's eviscerated schematism, we find that remoter effects are seldom aimed at by causal intentions, that no one kind of causal activity continues indefinitely.[1]

*P*rofessor Bergson, though of course he ought to, does not believe anything of the sort, since the Heracleitan *devenir réel* is not so real to him as the *P*lotinian duration, which is also *eternity*,[2] and since the continuity, indivisibility, and substantiality of that transcendental and metaphysical change which is real duration, vital impulse, creative evolution, preclude utterly just these empirical descriptions of how change and activity do go on and novelties do arise. *H*is critique of intellectualism, indeed, points to a recognition of the purely empirical character of change, but this is always incidental, and underneath it always stands the firm assumption of the unity of duration, of its diversification into the two inverse movements of spirit, and of the composition of the world of actual experience by the confrontation of these two forces.

[1] *A Pluralistic Universe*, pp. 397, 398.
[2] Cf. I*ntroduction à la métaphysique*, and *supra*.

The main outlines of Bergson's thought are the main outlines of all transcendentalism. The main outlines of James's thought are not prefigured in the history of philosophy. Seeking to build no system, not even an eclectic one, he organizes no material in any particular way. *H*e speaks of pragmatism as a *mediator* between rationalism and empiricism, monism and pluralism. He accepts apriorities in thought when they confirm themselves empirically as such; and he rejects dogmas when they do not so confirm themselves.[1] His alliances with traditional empiricism are not stronger than his alliances with traditional idealism. His ultimate alignment must be, as he himself points out, with realism. "Radical empiricism . . . . has more affinities with natural realism than with the views of Berkeley or of Mill."[2] Indeed it is naïve *or logical realism*,[3] freed from

[1] Cf. *Principles of Psychology*, II, chap. xxviii.

[2] *Radical Empiricism*, p. 76.

[3] Cf. *Some Problems of Philosophy*, p. 106: "What I am affirming here is the platonic doctrine that concepts are singulars, that concept-stuff is inalterable, and that physical realities are constituted by the various concept-stuffs of which they 'partake.' It is known as 'logical realism' in the history of philosophy; and

intellectualistic bias, and restored to that integrity and impartiality of insight which is the source of all that is systematic or dominative in philosophic perception.

has usually been more favored by rationalistic than by empiricist minds. For rationalism, concept-stuff is primordial, and perceptual things are secondary in nature. The present book, which treats concrete percepts as primordial and concepts as of secondary origin, may be regarded as somewhat eccentric in its attempt to combine logical realism with otherwise empiricist mode of thought."

CHAPTER V

DIVINITY, ITS NATURE AND ITS RÔLE IN HUMAN AFFAIRS

Is there, or can there be, in a world such as James sees, place for superhuman spirits, for the gods, for God?

In our biographies, essentially a sensational flux, chaotic, multiform, overrich in orders, this world makes of our minds

at every stage a theatre of simultaneous possibilities. Consciousness [in the revised and only acceptable sense of the term, i.e., in the sense of a specific sort of relation] consists in the comparison of these with each other, the selection of some and the suppression of the rest by the reinforcing and inhibiting agency of attention. The highest and most elaborate mental products are filtered from the data chosen by the faculty next beneath, out of the mass offered by the faculty below that, which mass in turn was sifted from a still larger amount of yet simpler material, and so on. The mind, in short, works on the data it receives, very much as a sculptor works on his block of stone. In a sense the statue stood there from all eternity. But there were a thousand different ones beside it, and the sculptor alone is to thank for having extricated this one from the

rest. Just so the world of each of us, howsoever different our several views of it may be, all lay imbedded
in the primordial chaos of sensations which gave the
mere *matter* to the thought of all of us indifferently.
We may, if we like, by our reasonings unwind things
back to that black and jointless continuity of space
and moving clouds of swarming atoms which science
calls the only real world. But all the while, the world
we feel and live in will be that which our ancestors and
we, by slowly cumulative strokes of choice, have extricated out of this, like sculptors, by simply rejecting
certain portions of the given stuff. Other sculptors,
other statues from the same stone! Other minds,
other worlds from the same monotonous and inexpres-
sive chaos! My world is but one of a million alike
imbedded, alike real to those who may abstract them.
How different must be the worlds in the mind of eel,
cuttle-fish, or crab![1]

*D*ifferent, but equally real! The insistent
metaphysical democratism dominates the
province of pure psychology also. And it is
from this that it reaches finally to the ultimate
walls of the world. For the psychological
region is the region of appreciation and judgment, par excellence, and judgment and appreciation would never be made if there were no
life to conserve, no environment to adapt, no

[1] *Principles of Psychology*, I, 288–89.

chaos to organize for the sake of that life.   If, then, interest compels us to select and selection generates practice and practice molds our originally plastic and indifferent alertness into *habit*, gradually reducing the give-and-take of our characters, hardening them into fixed orders and definitely articulate processes, is there not reason to believe that a similar consummation goes on in every entity that exists, living or inert, conscious or torpid?   Each has the same passive resistance to change, each offers similarly a certain active response to environment, each determines its environment, be it ever so little, with reference to *itself* as center, and from its own view carves out a world. The foot molds itself to the shoe as much as the shoe to the foot, the road and the driver to the automobile as much as the automobile to the driver and the road.   We see habits forming everywhere—everywhere an original foreignness and plasticity, everywhere a growing intimacy and interaccommodation and hardening; everywhere diversity passing into union and union into novel differentiations bred by

the very habit which is this union. If, then,
we take the evolutionary hypothesis radically
enough, we see a struggle for survival, an
activity of selection, a constant unification
by adaptation, and a diversification by spontaneous variation, throughout the entire range
of being. The universe, in a word, is tychistic.
Chance is real in it. Destruction is as possible
as salvation, and evil is as actual as good.
What is central is the fact that evil and good
are *relations*, and not substances, that each
entity which struggles can of itself and in its
own right contribute to the everlasting damna-
tion or eternal salvation of the world. There
is no eternal law; there is no over-arching
destiny, no all-compelling *P*rovidence. Law
itself is no more than cosmic habit, a *modus
vivendi*, which things that have come together
by chance, and are staying together by choice,
have worked out as men work out communal
customs facilitating contacts. Whether gravi-
tation or tobacco-smoking, there is a difference
in scope, not in history! And the spontaneous individualities whose collective habits the

"laws of nature" express are greater and more real than those laws. These individualities in their privacy and inwardness are reals in the completest sense of the term, and through them the axis of larger being runs. How otherwise should the history of the cosmos unfold itself? *H*ow be read?

If . . . . one takes the theory of evolution radically, one ought to apply it not only to the rock-strata, the animals, and the plants, but to the stars, to the chemical elements, to the laws of nature. There must have been a far-off antiquity, one is then tempted to suppose, when things were really chaotic. Little by little, and out of the haphazard possibilities of that time, a few connected things and habits arose, and the rudiments of regular performance began. Every variation in the way of law and order added itself to this nucleus, which inevitably grew more considerable as history went on; while the aberrant and inconstant variations, not being similarly preserved, disappeared from being, wandered off as unrelated vagrants, or else remained so imperfectly connected with the part of the world that had grown regular as only to manifest their existence by occasional lawless intrusions. . . . . Wisps and shreds of the original chaos, they would be connected enough with the cosmos to affect its periphery now and then, as by a momentary whiff or touch or gleam, but not enough ever to be followed up and hunted down and bagged. Their relation to the cosmos would be tangential solely.[1]

Superhuman minds are, clearly, not impossible in a world like this. They are admissible *ab origine;* they are admissible as evolutionary growths or as spontaneous variations. Their *naturalness* in reality is not in question: what is in question is their *nature*. What is their specific nature? What is their status? *Do* they belong to the steadily consolidating co-operative cosmos, or are they tangential, momentary whiffs and touches? *Do* they work? and good? or ill? How do they enter the world's *natural constitution*, keeping *single* the field of experience and the cosmos unsplit into a realm of nature and a realm of grace? What difference do they make in that constitution? How would it be otherwise, if they did not exist?

Since, at least for us human beings, reality resides in the parts more deeply and finally than in the whole, since the immediacies of experience, of the *here* and *now*, are in the pro-

[1] *Memories and Studies*, pp. 192, 193.

foundest sense the models of whatever other organizations of the real we choose to pursue, it is clear that superhuman consciousnesses must attach themselves in their own way to our individual lives, as do all the objects that interest selects out of the chaos to transvalue into a cosmos. Now these things, James finds, are what religious objects do supremely, and the inward life itself seems never so near reality as in religious experience. "By being religious we establish ourselves in possession of ultimate reality at the only points at which reality is given us to guard,"[1] and religion, hence, "occupying herself with personal destinies and keeping thus in contact with the only absolute realities we know, must necessarily play a part in human history."[2] So far as mankind is concerned, then, the religious object is integral to the human cosmos. Whether the gods be tangential to the world in its democratic indifference or no, they are not tangential to the destiny of man and must ever belong to

[1] *Varieties of Religious Experience*, p. 501.
[2] *Ibid.*, p. 503.

that one of the equally real millions of worlds which we carve out, for the sake of our interests and the filling of our needs, from the boundless sensational flux.

The gods reside, then, at least to our belief, far down with those depths of feeling which are the core of our reality and the very seat and *go* of what is individual and personal, or what is real. But this residence is not sufficient to establish their status. Tables and chairs, number-systems, fairies, and vain imaginings reside there, too. Concepts have a fireside corner in that inwardness. It is itself multifold and chaotic, and the order of its being as various as the strands that comprise it. The gods may be, like concepts, *consubstantial* with percepts, with actual tables and tangible chairs, and still be derivative and secondary functions, mere *meanings* whose whole significance is in their prophetic outcome, not in their active and individuate being. Indeed, the reality of the concept "God" is just such a *functional* reality, the reality of a tendency in our private natures, of a "faith-state," rather than of a living impelment in an independent object, existing by the primacy of its own will, maintaining that existence by its own force, and claiming it as its own metaphysical right. Such an existence would not be truly individual and real. It would be a member but not an efficacy in the cosmos. Its force would be the force of the human personality which bred it, its place the place which that personality assigned it. Not quite tangential, neither would it be altogether integral in the cosmos. Its position would be peripheral without being beyond the reach of the influences radiating from the center.

The locus of the gods or of God is, however, much more nearly central than that, and their reality is profoundly more solid. Infrequently though, and at the cost of however much order and peace, they *do* appear; their reality, when it does reveal itself, reveals itself in ways overmastering. *Perceived* essentially not otherwise than our fellows and things are perceived, they operate, through our perception of them, the transvaluation of all our values, the reconstruction and reordering of our private worlds. It then seems as if we were the chisels and they sculptors, and the systems they carve with and for and through us seem infinitely righter and better than those we had carved for ourselves. They renew the heavens, they renew the earth, they renew the human heart.

Their mode of renewal is not yet well studied. Its existence is established, its strongest features are known, its operations are explicable. It is not an interruption of the world's order, but a reassurance and continuation of it. The science of the psychologist may, within narrow limits, exhibit and analyze it. But its outcome escapes except in works.

Concretely, the mode is knowledge-of-acquaintance. But its content is so enormously ineffable that the directness and immediacy of apprehension which constitutes its psychologic nature is overshadowed by this other quality. It is commonly regarded not as a knowledge at all, but as a mystery. There is sufficient reason for such a regard, seeing that the powers of perception which touch and apprehend it are not those of daily use, and that their activity, indeed, often requires the suspension of those in daily use. Massive somatic reflexes seem often at work; the "higher centers" seem independently energetic. There is implicated, in a word, a condition of neural tension in which the customary modes of discharge, on the ordinary levels of sensation and perception, have somehow been abolished—perhaps through anesthetics, perhaps through ritual and purificatory exercises, perhaps through no known natural cause—or have not yet re-established themselves. Consciousness, the while, is present and reaches into regions not comparable with the known ones of the daily life. This consciousness seems deeper, seems to reside on levels lower down and more extensive than those of the self of waking life, to reside on "subconscious" levels, and there it appears to be preternaturally alert and explicit. What it is awake to and apprehends is, by report which as little as anything else in the world is open to question, *spirit*. And in the apprehension of this spirit

consists the mystic experience.[1] This experience is multifold in its objects and manifestations,[2] exceedingly varied in its consequences
and complicated in its connections, as full of
contradictions and enmities reconciled and
active as is the sensory flux. "They do not
contradict these facts [already objectively
before us] as such or deny anything that our
senses have immediately seized."[3] They are
additive to the rest of experience, their effect
being *revaluative*, not transubstantiative. They
enter through a region in our nature

that is obviously the larger part of each of us, for it is
the abode of everything that is latent and the reservoir
of everything that passes unrecorded or unobserved.
It contains, for example, such things as all our momen-
tarily inactive memories, and it harbors the springs
of all our obscurely motived passions, impulses, likes,
dislikes, and prejudices. Our intuitions, hypotheses,
fancies, superstitions, persuasions, convictions, and, in
general, all our non-rational operations come from it.
It is the source of our dreams, and apparently they
may return to it. In it arise whatever mystical experiences we may have, and our automatisms, sensory

[1] Cf. *Varieties of Religious Experience*, chapter on "Mysti-
cism," particularly pp. 504-6.

[2] *Ibid.*, p. 425.   [3] *Ibid.*, p. 427.

or motor; our life in hypnotic and "hypnoid" conditions, if we are subject to such conditions; our delusions, fixed ideas, and hysterical accidents, if we are hysteric subjects; our supranormal cognitions if such there be, and if we are telepathic subjects. It is also the fountainhead of much that feeds our religion. In persons deep in the religious life, as we have abundantly seen, ... the door into this region seems unusually wide open; at any rate, experiences making their entrances through that door have had emphatic influence in shaping religious history.[1]

Spirit then, pours into the daily life through the funnel of the subconscious, and in a fellowship which prejudices its acknowledgment and does it otherwise no good. But be its fellowship the most favorable and commending, it must still "be sifted and tested and run the gauntlet of confrontation with the total context of experience, just like what comes from the outer world of sense." Such sifting and testing reveals that it may be evil and diabolical, the enemy of life; as well as good and divine, the conserving friend of life.[2] It wears, in a word, the same significance for our interests as the other entities of experience, and is not

[1] *Ibid.*, pp. 483, 484.   [2] *Ibid.*, p. 426.

confined to being merely propitious. It has a nature and destiny of its own, and its bearing toward humanity, like the bearing of men toward each other, may in no small degree be determined by mankind's bearing toward the destiny of such supranormal spirits. The relation of the two is moral; there is, empirically, a conventional give-and-take. The "mystic" *behaves* otherwise than an environment not containing spirit would require. *H*e acknowledges its actual presence, he seeks union or harmonious relations with it as his true end, and, in his contact with it, in prayer or inner communion, "work is really done, and spiritual energy flows in and produces effects, psychological or material, within the phenomenal world." And all this at just these points where reality is felt at its glowing fulness of force and presence, in the concrete immediacy of individual experience as such. There, in all religious experience, among all peoples, in all times, in all places, the individual "becomes conscious that . . . . [this] higher part is conterminous and continuous with a *more* of the same quality, which is operative in the universe outside of him, and which he can keep in working touch with and in a fashion get on board of, and save himself when all his lower being has gone to pieces in the wreck."

There underlies here the assumption that the "more" and the mystic have a *common aim*, in so far forth, and the assurance that they are of identical substance. Concerning the specific nature of this substance there is disagreement. Some find just a "stream of ideal tendency," others genuine and differing personalities; but all find it dynamic, dynamogenic, efficacious. Subtract the quarrels of creeds and schools, and what remains is "literally and objectively true" and "what remains" is this: "the conscious person is continuous with a wider self through which saving experiences come," continuous without being depersonalized, coactive without being absorbed. The relation is external as well as internal. Religion in the strict sense of the term is an empirical instance of the "compounding of consciousness" which we saw to be so central in the Jamesian apprehension of reality.[1]

These unhuman, superior, and saving consciousnesses are of course *finite*, and certainly not reducible to one. The facts exhibit a "supernaturalism" which is not universalistic, but "piecemeal," and whatever the power or the status of the supranormal spirits, they live in an environment with which they must cope even as man must with his, and they too work for a salvation which has the *chance* of being lost as well as attained. Men and gods may be fellow-soldiers in a struggle to banish evil from the world, to make reality over into a complete cosmos. Whatever the extent of the world may be, gods, not otherwise than men, are less than it. Both empirically and dialectically, there is a residuum which is different and additive, with which gods must cope as man does. And in this struggle, men may help gods perhaps as much as gods help men. "Who knows whether the faithfulness of individuals here below to their own poor over-

[1] *Supra*, chaps. ii and iv.

beliefs, may not actually help God in turn to be more effectively faithful to his own greater tasks ?"[1]

From the standpoint of radical empiricism, then, in a world having the history and the constitution the world of radical empiricism shows itself to possess, superhuman consciousness is not merely not ruled out by hypothesis; it is established by experience as immediate and as coercive as any other experience men base deductions on. It is additive to the routinal content of the daily life, but integrally additive; no momentary whiff or touch; entering the normal constitution of the world by way of the "subliminal" self, and working through it both evil and good, but chiefly good. And this conclusion is born of no dialectical analysis, no syllogistic deduction. It is an inductive summary of recorded fact.

Quite the contrary in the Bergsonian philosophy. Bergson nowhere directly faces the problems put by religious experience as such, nor does he consider that the content of

---

[1] *Varieties of Religious Experience*, p. 519.

religious emotion is different from the content
revealed in the intuition of anything moving
and active.   Of the uniqueness, the persistence,
and the significance of the "religious sentiment" he is convinced. It belongs to the
profundities of our nature. The ideas in
religion, on the contrary, are external. One
gives way to another; none endures.[1] They
are mere symbols of a deeper thing. But is
this deeper thing "God"? Is it a "more"
like ourselves from which men may draw,
in their need, aid and comfort? A thing
warm and intimate and personal, in the
human sense of "personal"? One can hardly
say so.

The considerations [writes Bergson in a letter to
a friend[2]] set forth in my "essay" on the immediate
data of consciousness are intended to bring to light
the fact of liberty; those in *Matter and Memory* touch
upon the reality of spirit; those in *Creative Evolution*
present creation as a fact. From all this, there clearly
emerges the idea of a God, creator and free; the gen-
erator at once of matter and of life, whose creative
efforts as regards life are continued through the evo-

[1] Cf. Charpin, *La question religieuse.*
[2] Printed by E. LeRoy in *Une philosophie nouvelle.*

lution of species and the constitution of human personalities.

Such a god is a totality. That his nature is spiritual need not be argued. But his spirit is not the spirit which is manifest in the daily life. The daily life is spatial and this spirit is disengaged from space. It is the spirit revealed in intuition, the common, impersonal psyche, both subhuman and transhuman, which is the *go* in all going things. It is the *élan vital*. Not, however, the *élan* revealed in the manifest movement of existence here and now. As such, it is limited and inhibited by its opposite, matter. For "life is a movement, materiality is the inverse movement, and each of these two movements is simple, the matter which forms a world being an undivided flux, and undivided also the life that runs through it, cutting out in it living beings all along its track."[1] The "God, creator and free," must be something "vaster and higher," the eternal spring of both matter and life. The whole universe reveals the force which mounts and

[1] *Creative Evolution*, p. 299.

the force which falls, and the movement is as
from a center, "a center from which worlds
shoot out like rockets in a fireworks display."
This center is God. God is not a thing,
but a "continuity of shooting-out." "*H*e has
nothing of the ready-made; he is unceasing
life, action, freedom." Unbounded by any
environment, it is the utterly indeterminate
spontaneity of becoming, self-contained and
self-limited, hence in the traditional sense of
the word, *infinite*. It is only "the force which
is evolving throughout the organized world"
that is a limited force, that is always seeking
to transcend itself, that is always inadequate
to its own aspirations. The center from which
this force springs has not these limitations.
It is the making, indifferently, of both matter
and *élan*, and its bearing on human destiny
therefore cannot with any honesty be said to
be propitious. It is both the enemy and the
friend, whereas the *élan* alone is utterly good,
utterly a saving "more." Thus:

Life appears in its entirety as an immense wave
which, starting from a center, spreads outward, and

which at almost the whole of its circumference is stopped and converted into oscillation: at one single point the obstacle has been forced, the impulsion has passed freely. It is this freedom that the human form registers. Everywhere but in man, consciousness has come to a stand; in man alone it has kept on its way. Man, then, continues the vital movement indefinitely, although he does not draw along with him all that life carries in itself. On other lines of evolution there have travelled other tendencies which life implied, and of which, since everything interpenetrates, man has doubtless kept something, but of which he has kept very little. *It is as if a vague and formless being, whom we may call as we will,* man, *or* superman, *had sought to realize himself and had succeeded only by abandoning a part of himself on the way.* . . . .

From this point of view, the discordances of which nature offers us the spectacle are singularly weakened. The organized world as a whole becomes the soil on which was to grow either man himself or a being who morally must resemble him. The animals, however distant they may be from our species, however hostile to it, have none the less been useful travelling companions on whom consciousness has unloaded whatever encumbrances it was dragging along and who have enabled it to rise, in man, to heights from which it sees an unlimited horizon open again before it.[1]

The *élan*, then, is good on the whole. That evils exist is not denied, but their source is not

[1] *Ibid.*, pp. 266, 267.

the *élan* itself.   Their source is the obstruction
that the *élan* meets.   This always opposes it,
turns it aside, divides it.   For this *élan*, being
finite, cannot overcome all obstacles, and the
conflict with those obstacles comprises organic
evolution.   This is individuation of the initial
impetus which has been given once for all, and
individuation with its consequent individualities are the basis and the source of evil.   Each
species thinks only for itself and lives only for
itself, creating thus the "numberless struggles
that occur in nature," the "discord as striking
as it is terrible."   But for this discord "the
*original principle of life must not be held respon-
sible.*"[1]

The original principle of life!   Not, however, God, the central source of this principle;
the central source of its enemy, matter;   in
whom both of these are one;   between whom
and man they move in ascending and descending hierarchies.   Man seems to be the cosmic
destiny by the cosmos' own choice, the goal and
pinnacle of creation, the very image of God.

[1] *Ibid.*, p. 255.   Italics mine.

And yet this god, if god it is, is a finite and lesser god, and the goodness of the ascending flux of spirit with which man's spirit is coincident in intuition is counterbalanced and overweighed by the evil of the descending flux of matter, the great enemy of essential man. The opposing flux seems to be of an inverse order, the devil, a machine; while the great source of both is a center of indifference morally, quite as much as it is a center of continuous creation.

*H*ence, Bergson seems on the one hand to entertain conceptions that are hardly to be distinguished from orthodox theism, and, in so far forth, to be in *tendency* (only in tendency) of the same opinion as James. He asserts the probability of a Fechnerian hierarchy of beings, one within the other. There exist, he argues, objects both inferior and superior to us, although, nevertheless, in a certain sense, within us. Intuition reveals their harmonious existence. Once you instal yourself by an act of intuition within the heart of duration, you cannot help perceiving this. For all intuition is of the same genus, no doubt, but of different species. And each species is identical with a distinct degree of being. These degrees you perceive in intuition. You are there possessed by the perception of a certain very definite durational tension, and its definiteness has the appearance of a choice among an infinity of possible durations. Thence you perceive as many durations as you please, each different from its fellows, and all different from each other. They constitute, however, a Bergsonian continuity, a continuity which you may follow, whether up or down. The pursuit will cost you enormous effort; it requires you to do violence to your normal selfhood. But the reward of violence is an expansion in which you transcend your normal selfhood. You may move *down*, from quality to quantity, to the pure repetition by which matter is designated, or up, to eternity. The movement is without a joint or break, an ineffable, interpenetrating many-in-one. Its uppermost limit is not the barren and inert eternity of Spinoza's God but rather the overflowing goodness of *Philo's* and Plotinos'. It is "a living, ever-moving eternity, where we find our own duration, as vibrations are found in light, and eternity which is the concretion of all duration just as matter is its deglutition."[1] And this absolute, concrete eternity embracing *both* matter and spirit is the greatest God of all. God, so defined, however, is an utter totality. It is prior to the degrees and steps of duration, both the subhuman and the transhuman, by coincidence with which man attains its completeness. From it all these derive; upon it, all depend; while in itself it is external to nothing and depends upon nothing.

So that, on the other hand, the Bergsonian vision soars to an utter God of gods whose total immanence constitutes the reality of all that is. *H*erein it allies itself with historic idealism and monism, with the radical anti-

[1] Cf. *Introduction à la métaphysique*, pp. 20, 25.

orthodox position concerning the nature of religion's God. This position is and has ever been the position of the philosophic tradition. It makes no consummation of the common report of many men. It abandons the experiential records of that daily life which communes with the gods. It reconstitutes the latter into a transcendental totality which becomes the subject of dialectic discourse. It identifies religion with philosophy. And this, in the end, is what Bergson does. "Intuition moves between these two extreme limits [matter and eternity] and this movement is metaphysics itself."[1]

Touching the moral bearings of the intermediate durations, their ultimate relation to man and his destiny, Bergson says explicitly nothing. There are only the hints concerning the goodness of the *élan* as a whole, the tendency of each degree to think only of itself, and the consequent evil. May not a wider duration think only of itself? and therefore, even though spirit, be the enemy of man? And

[1] Cf. *Introduction à la métaphysique*, p. 25.

is not the all-good *élan* itself, favoring man as such, yet *as a whole,* if not *on the whole,* the enemy of each and every one of its parts? What is the destiny of man if the world be as Bergson describes it? And what, if it be as James describes it?

CHAPTER VI

THE ORIGIN AND DESTINY OF MAN

If the feeling of substantial identity with the all-creative force be religious feeling, if the perception of that identity in intuition be religious experience, if the designation of that force as good on the whole be religious assurance, if the characterization of man as the implicit goal of creative evolution be religious providence, then Bergson is orthodoxly religious, in the essential sense of the term. There are difficulties, however, as we have seen, in reconciling this conception with whatever explicit statements concerning the nature of God Bergson has made. If the *élan vital* is God, then the universal center of creation from which springs matter (peer of the *élan*), is a super-god. And if what is overt and distinctive in human nature is at a qualitatively far remove from the *élan*, how much more alien must it be to the "center of continuous creation"!

There is an inevitable antithesis and opposition between what is distinctly human and
what is cosmic. It is the abandonment of its
humanity, not the bold and convinced maintenance of it, that reunites our spirit with the
cosmic spirit. Intuition is an "inversion"
of the most determinate and fixed direction
of the overt life, a rupture of the most "cherished habits" of the soul. What is uniquely
human in us, our intelligence, is the very stuff
and being of matter, not of spirit. None the
less, in man the *élan* has freed itself from the
restrictions and opposition of matter, and men
are free wills, integrally and completely creative,
renewers, the paragons of earth! A contradiction, this? Not necessarily. Just because
God is the flowing of spirit and matter at one
and the same time; just because in God these
streams cross and combat one another; just
because all reality is this immense dualism,
there is no life whose nature is an individuation
of the cosmical *élan* which, by that very fact,
does not deeply and completely participate in
the dualism, and man more than all. For

man is a microcosm. He images the world. In him, corresponding to the spirit and matter of the universal cosmos, are instinct and intelligence, with intelligence dominant. Indeed he does live and move and have his being in the absolute. And for that very reason, the truly *he* of *him*, the differentiae that constitute his humanity, are mere appearance, and his individuality is a thing secondary, not primary. It is primary only in his selfishness and egocentricity, only because he regards himself as the be-all and end-all of this cosmic evolution. Bergson does not disapprove this self-regarding attitude. Indeed he may be said to warrant it by his designation of man as the cosmic goal. But he holds it to be none the less the source of all evil, and pure good to be only in the unindividuated totality of the *élan*.

What then is the nature of human individuality? What its status? What its destiny?

The cosmic life, confronted and opposed by matter, seeks to break through the obstruction, to overcome it, to abolish it. But abolition is impossible; matter is as durable as life. Life proceeds, therefore, by "insinuating" itself into matter, by even adopting matter's rhythms, by so molding, organizing, shaping matter that its geometric rigidity becomes flexible, that its determination becomes indetermination, its necessity as nearly freedom as may be. The goal of life is its own free mobility. The enemy of that mobility is matter. *H*ence the work of life is the conquest of matter. Organic existence in all its ranges of kind and complexity is just so many experiments which life makes in the conquest of matter, just so many attempts at escape from the material prison in which life finds itself inclosed. For this reason, living bodies represent, in the light of the intention and potency of life, so many obstacles avoided, not so many tasks achieved. By means of none, however, are obstacles so completely avoided as by means of the central nervous system in man, particularly by his brain. The brain is a very "center of indetermination." It presents to the psychic stream an enormous variety of paths of discharge, and it allows the stream of consciousness to be at each moment of its flow an inward fiat, undetermined by the brain's mechanical constitution; a chosen movement, unique, novel, simple, in an unforeseeable direction along one of the countless paths of discharge which comprise the central structure.

The consciousness so arising and so perceived is not any longer, however, that cosmic spirit, multiple yet interpenetratively one, which is opposed to matter, matter being no less than life an undivided flux, but "weighted with geometry." This consciousness is quite another thing, and its existence means a specific modification of the flux of both matter and spirit. Each of these is a continuance. But the continuity of spirit is cumulative, spirit endures and grows; while the continuity of matter is conservative, matter redistributes and repeats. Spiritual action elapses; material action is instantaneous. Consequently spirit is free, creative, unique from pulse to pulse; matter is mechanical, repetitive, common, and the same from pulse to pulse. Both, in their totality, are impersonal. The evolution of organic life is personalization of the impersonal. In the person, life has given up some of its spontaneity, matter some of its rigidity, and personification is the process of this mutual interaccommodation.

The two encounter each other first in "pure perception." This is the direct contact of spirit and matter, a contact unindividualized and universal. Life's task, if it is to vanquish in this encounter, must be to overcome the inertia of matter, to delay the mechanical and ceaseless repetition of the same which is matter's action, to prolong this action from instantaneity to duration. If it can do this, it can open an outlet in matter through which consciousness may flow. And it does do this in organic bodies, particularly in human bodies, with their infinitely complex brains. The organic body is cut out and set somewhat apart from the cosmic continuity of matter; it has a freedom of movement and activity which the non-organic does not possess; and more particularly, it has a liberty of response that inorganic bodies do not possess. The latter are compelled to react to and to transmit any action that they receive in a predetermined direction and a fixed mode. Not so organic bodies. And most completely not so the human body with its central nervous system. This, indeed, is nothing but a "center of inde-termination." In it reaction is not immediate, but suspended; activity accumulates, gets turned into the *potential* action of the body. But this accumulating and enduring activity is life, is spirit itself, set free from the self-annulling instantaneity of reaction which is matter. Yet it is no longer, on this level, the pure transcendental spirit. On this level, it is spirit literally incarnate, personalized; and the incarnation and personification have con-sisted in the *enchannelment* of the cumu-lative activity within the motor organs of the body. So enchanneled, it exists as the consciousness we feel in the daily life. It is nothing more than the *potential action* of the physical organism, nothing more than the outline of this action, reflected back upon the material continuum whence the action came.

Personification, then, is, in its first phase, limitation, enchannelment. There is to be found in it, on the level of pure perception, something more akin to matter than to spirit. It is no more than the spirit in matter, liberated. Complete personality, however, demands more than that. It demands biography, intimacy, memory. And these are what is supplied. For the incoming activity, which, by means of the brain, is arrested and accumulated, looks not only back to its source, in the character of the form of the body's potential reaction to that source, it looks also inward to the creative spirit which is the *life* of the body. At the same time that it outlines in matter, as a reflection, our eventual action upon it, it is also reflected in memory, and there dissolved into spirit and sucked down below the level of consciousness. Now this dual movement has required changes in the body, and these changes are copresent. Consciousness feels them. It feels them to be quite different from *memory* or *perception*, neither the outline of an action that may be, nor the quality of an action that has been. They are a *real* action, "the permanent and unique" factor in that group of "images" with which the needs of consciousness are concerned. To this, then, both perception and memory attach themselves, and when they are so attached, the triad constitutes a "person." *P*erception reaches outward into matter; memory inward to spirit; in the action of the body, these two mingle their lights, and spirit overcomes the resistance of matter. One's body is thus a center *in* which there flows a congeries of accumulating possibilities of action; *about* which there floats the integrate fusion of one's history in the unity of one's past, the condensation of one's history. For memory, let me repeat, is perception joining spirit instead of going back to matter. It "doubles perception" and conserves itself automatically, though subconsciously. It is narrowed down to personality, is kept distinct and individual by being attached to the body. Each unique item of one's unique past is a *guide* directing the motor mechanisms of the nervous system. The body's needs raise it from the level of the unconscious past to that of the conscious present, materialize it; nor is there anything more in the present than the feelings of the body and of the guiding memories taking form through its needs.

The consciousness of our lives from day to day, it follows, the selfhood that is near and characteristic and individual and personal is always *the present.* Whatever it contains that is truly *unique* and *other*, truly individual, depends upon the body, which alone can invoke the images of memory from the depths of the subconscious, the impersonal spirit, which is pure activity. But such a recalling is an exteriorization of what is interpenetrative and one. It is a spatialization of spirit. *H*ence our life proceeds on an artificial and superficial level, and the very quality of our natures makes it impossible for us naturally to apprehend the spiritual reality from which we derive.

For emphatically, what personalizes is that only which constitutes our present. And that is the feeling of the body's action. The impersonal is dragged out of its interpenetrative retreat to serve the needs of this action. Individuality is physical, hence spatial. Whatever relates to it, therefore, must be equally spatial. In consequence our daily life, as described by empirical psychology, can be described in terms of habit, of association, of reflection. None of these terms applies to the depths of spirit. All apply to the levels of matter. What is distinctive about us is non-spiritual.

How should this be, about us, in whom, as Bergson tells us repeatedly, spirit has broken the wall of matter and flows freely? It is because, in us, spirit has had "to adopt matter's very rhythms," to *become* matter. For what distinguishes man from other living creatures? Intelligence. And what is intelligence if not an essential geometry in its form, and an essential capacity to handle *unorganized bodies, to construct machines*, in its process. Geometry is the analysis of space, and space, the opposite of spirit, is the complete externality of points to one another, of points different merely in number, but in substance homogeneous. Its essence, therefore, is the repetition of identities, and this is the dominant principle of the "identity-logic," which is the *form* of intelligence. We think differents in terms of *the same*, always; our intellect can rearrange reality but can never discover anything new in it, nor deal with it in its totalities, as do creatures highly endowed with instincts, such as ants, bees, wasps, and women. Compare man with the other animals and you find that, on the one hand, he is, of all, least protected by nature and structure against the environment, while, on the other hand, he alone has organs not attached by *specific* function to a restricted environment. Man's hands are free. *H*e has and exercises the capacity of using the material environment by manufacturing unorganized instruments of it, supplying himself out of it with what nature doesn't endow him: defense, shelter, food.

To do this, man must *understand* and *know* his environment. But this environment is matter, and such understanding and knowing must be an adaptation to the habits of matter. Thus intelligence, in its *use*, is the insinuation of spirit into matter, the adoption of its rhythm and character. Intelligence is conscious materiality in action. It will tend, therefore, to establish relations, such as the Kantian categories, by means of which things are external one to another—categories of equivalence, whole and part, causation, and so on. Intelligence is and *acts* the Kantian architectonic, the regulative principles of "pure reason." It is not, however, added to space from the outside, but derived from space from the inside. Its forms and principles do, therefore, rightly constitute the presupposition of the inventive genius of man, the *homo faber*, and are the actual framework of the physicist's world of matter and space. In intelligence, spirit and matter are identical, and spirit even exceeds matter in its movement toward space. For matter never quite geometrizes; its content and form never become absolutely spatial; they exceed and deviate from the precision of law, their reality is never quite grasped by science. In intelligence, consequently, spirit completely inverts itself, where in matter spirit only partly inverts itself. What is most distinctive of man is least distinctive of the *élan vital;* what is individual is unreal. In the creative current of life the individual is only an excrescence on the essential progress which is the heart of life; a mere channel and thoroughfare, the essence of whose living resides in the movement by which life is transmitted. Race and individual, what is different and distinct in them, are accidental and relatively unreal in the universe. Beside the creative center, the flux of life, the downrush of matter, the totality of organic beings, these former are unrealities, mere appearance, the superficies and last steps of becoming, not its deep and throbbing heart, not the "need to create."

*H*owever, let no hopeful and aspiring mind fall to despair thereby. Ephemeral incident though the individual be, the undivided, indivisible, creative onrush that belittles him also glorifies and saves him. The inward will to live in man is deceived by no illusion of immortality; even in his altogether partitive and individuate being, the *élan* has prefigured and shall perhaps continue him without the body. For in the corporate body of humanity, spirit possesses a machine which triumphs over mechanism; in the brain, in language, in social life, man has instruments that make for an ever greater and greater lability and spontaneity of action. And it is only as such a creative freedom that man has been prefigured, not formally and teleologically. *H*uman freedom, moreover, is not complete freedom; human consciousness is largely intellect; and the totality of freedom is not alone creative of matter, but of spirit also: to intellect must be added intuition. "A complete and perfect humanity would be that in which these two forms of conscious activity should attain their full development."[1] Such a humanity would possess in intuition all that is given

[1] *Creative Evolution*, p. 159.

to intellect and instinct both, *the deepest unity of the spiritual life.*[1]

Such a humanity will see "the life of the body just where it really is, on the road that leads to the life of the spirit." It will see the spirit there, as a rising wave, composed of innumerable interpenetrating potentialities, a continuous *élan*, neither one nor many. It will see this *élan* in its onrush, breaking up by force of the matter through which it flows into individuals, but individuals which "are vaguely indicated in it" and need the help of matter to become clear. They pre-exist, indeed, and yet are created. Matter helps them to pass from potentiality to actuality, and the body is this aid. And even as the individual was "vaguely indicated" before his incarnation in matter, so, enriched by his experience in the body, he may go on, after his separation from the body; "the destiny of consciousness . . . . is not bound up with the destiny of cerebral matter."[2] Indeed, in the attack of life upon matter, "the whole of

[1] *Ibid.*, p. 267.　　　[2] *Ibid.*, p. 270.

humanity in space and time is one immense army galloping beside and before and behind each of us in an overwhelming charge able to beat down every resistance and to clear the most formidable obstacles, perhaps even death."[1]

So individuality is derived, justified, abolished and resurrected, all in one stroke of intuition. *P*urely a limitation and narrowing of the wider stream of spirit which is life itself, an excrescence and excess, its status is altogether secondary and representative. It holds neither strength nor excellence in its own right: all its goodness comes to it by grace of the "larger life" from which matter breaks it, and all its goodness must to that life return: to find itself it must deny itself. The intuition is contradictory, but eminently satisfactory in its compensatory import.

Now to William James nothing could be more repugnant than a conception of individuality like this. To him the pre-existence or the postexistence of individuals was largely

[1] *Op. cit.*, p. 271.

unimportant. But individuality as such, whatever its origin or level, he held most precious. It is that which impresses him in Bergson himself: "Neither one of Taine's famous principles of explanations of great men, the *race,* the *environment, or the moment,* no, nor all three together will explain that peculiar way of looking at things that constitutes his mental individuality. Originality in men dates from nothing previous, other things date from it rather."[1] There is an absolute and irreducible *hæceitas* in individuality, foreshadowed not even dimly, furnished by neither matter nor spirit, but the very uniqueness and peculiarity of the particular life which is both, given *as* that uniqueness and peculiarity, which alone is the potent and operative thing in human life, determining its social direction and establishing its particular worth.

Its origin, consequently, is a matter of indifference. James assumes the *D*arwinian hypothesis, naturally: what is human in man is a spontaneous variation, a mutation upon

[1] *A Pluralistic Universe,* p. 226.

the subhuman surviving by force of its inward
power. What matters to him, however, is
this: that, whatever the origin of individuality, whether it be primary or derived, once it
it *occurs, it* is the thing that counts, not its
source. And it counts because there is in it
something absolute and *un*accountable, which
cannot be brought back to a "larger whole,"
a background, an environment, or a cause.
In that unaccountable differentia lie its force,
significance, and worth. What it is in its
uniqueness defies analysis. Generically it is
a dynamogenic activity of "appropriation"
whose center and "invariant" is the body, and
whose "continuous identity" as personal consciousness is "the practical fact that new experiences come which look back on the old ones,
find them "warm," and greet and appropriate
them as "mine." The "warmth" is a group
of somatic feelings of direction: that is, of
"attention," of "interest," of the vividness
and immediacy of motor consciousness. This
group is the I, the me, the central and nuclear
self, appropriation by which gives any entity

a personic status and a place in a biography.
The stuff of it is "constant play of further-
ances and hindrances in my thinking, of checks
and releases, of tendencies which run with
desire and tendencies which run the other
way. . . . . The mutual inconsistencies and
agreements, reinforcements and obstructions,
which obtain among these objective matters,
reverberate backward and produce what seems
to be incessant reactions of my spontaneity
upon them, welcoming or opposing, appropriating or disowning, striving with or against,
saying yes or no. This palpitating inward life
is . . . . that central nucleus,"[1] that core of
adjustments continually repeated, to all which
the stream of thought brings up. This "all" is
made up of parts as variable and conflicting
as the central core itself, and even more so;
and any harmonious congregations of such
parts may constitute a *self* which is both a
peer and in fact a dilemmatic alternative of
perhaps a hundred other such harmonious
congregations. Experience is thus always

[1] *Principles of Psychology*, I, 299.

saying to the individual *either-or;* "*either* millionaire *or* saint, *either bon vivant* or philanthropist: *either* philosopher *or* lady-killer." To the honest observer the mind is a theater of gregarious and struggling possibilities, all equal, but only one capable of realization at any time. Its individuality is constituted ultimately by that unique quality of fiat, which, throughout a life, chooses a realization of a determinate kind. Its identity maintains and reveals itself as the continuity of this act of choice, or, where discontinuity is felt, as resemblance of the discontinuities in some fundamental respect, for continuity and similarity carry onward the "warmth" and immediacy of the choosing or appropriating act. And selfhood is at its core exactly this *passing*, this appropriation, this choosing—a bridge between what *was* the warm and living I, and what *becomes* this I.

The universal conscious fact is not "feelings and thoughts exist," but "I think" and "I feel." No psychology, at any rate, can question the *existence* of personal selves. The worst a psychology can do is so to interpret the nature of these selves as to rob them of their worth. A French writer, speaking of our ideas, says somewhere, in a fit of anti-spiritualistic excitement, that, misled by certain peculiarities which they display, we "end by personifying" the procession which they make, such personification being regarded by him as a great philosophic blunder on our part. It could only be a blunder if the notion of personality meant something essentially different from anything to be found in the mental procession. But if the procession be itself the very "original" of the notion of personality, to personify it cannot possibly be wrong. It is already personified. There are no marks of personality to be gathered *aliunde* and then found lacking in the train of thought. It has them already, so that to whatever farther analysis we may subject that form of personal selfhood under which thoughts appear, it is, and must remain, true that the thoughts which psychology studies do continually tend to appear as parts of personal selves.[1]

The I or Ego is here not deduced, but discovered, as primary and immediate a datum of experience, at least, as any other, and in fact more primary and immediate *than* any other. Such accounts of *self* which the philosophic tradition gives, and Bergson's with them, are simply hypostases of some phase of the actual continuum of the "mental procession."

[1]*Principles*, I, 226 f.

The literature of the Self is large [writes James], but all its authors may be classed as radical or mitigated representatives of . . . . three schools . . . . substantialism, associationism, or transcendentalism. Our own opinion, must be classed apart, although it incorporates essential elements from all three schools. There need never have been a quarrel between associationism and its rival if the former had admitted the indecomposable unity of every pulse of thought[1] and the latter been willing to allow that "perishing" pulses of thought might recollect and know.[2]

Each Ego, then, consists of indecomposable pulses of thought—selections, recollections, and cognitions, operating together uniquely as an individual. It is a central and unceasing activity, a vortex of choosing, whose tendency and direction is the definitive constituent of character. It contains all that is empirically required to define the qualities and attributes of individuality and selfhood. There is no detachment from a greater mass, no individuation, no decrease; rather the opposite. Individuality is much more a synthesis, an integration, than an analysis, and what is

---

[1] It is this that Bergson hypostatizes.

[2] *Principles*, I, pp. 369 f.

most characteristic of it, therefore, is not intellect as the *form of matter*, but intellect as the *facile movement of spirit;* intellect, consequently, not as a mere substitution for reality but as the very creative act, the inventiveness, of the human spirit. Therein it is that those great ideas grow which afterward become the organizing concepts of scientific systems; there, in a chaos of variations, both spontaneous and caused, from which the lower and more durable levels of existence afterward select—some, to conserve and to perpetuate; some, to destroy. There is the zone of insecurity, the formative zone of conscious life and growth; the seat, hence, of all the progress that mankind knows. Not the immediate push of society or the remoter onrush of an *élan,* but the constant choices of the individual, urge humanity forward. The *fiat* of belief that asserts its object before it is assured of the being of that object, the inward "need to create," the demand for rationality in the individual soul as that soul reveals itself empirically—these and these alone are sufficient to alter and direct the movement of the universe and the destiny of man.[1]

The pluralistic insistence on individuality runs, we have seen, through all of James's thinking. It is perhaps nowhere so clear as in his utterances concerning the ultimate destiny of man. Morally, he urges over and again, not less than metaphysically, reality is a multiverse. There is a warfare of moral ideals. No part of existence was made *for* any other part; each is concerned primarily with itself, and tends to appropriate the others in the interests of its selfhood. The struggle for survival is ontological. It is the quality of existence through and through, so that portions of reality may be easily lost altogether beyond the shadow of a possibility of redemption. A pluralism with time as its force, the world reveals nothing absolutely fixed, nothing absolutely certain. Risk attaches to everything: even the most firm "universal" proposition involves a dangerous leap beyond evidence.

[1] Cf. "The Importance of Individuals" in *The Will to Believe*, etc.

Every doubt is a conflict in beliefs; every belief a bridge thrust across a darkness of ignorance, and the other shore, the shore of "fact" it is intended to reach, may not exist.

Now overtly, the intimate essence of life is belief, belief being literally preference, choice, and the risk attached to believing. And beliefs are fertile and germinative; often they breed out of their very substance the object to which they attach, nowhere so much as in social relations. Social facts exist in virtue of the "precursive faith in one another of those immediately concerned." The wish is father to the fact. And in our constant struggle for life, and amid the ever-present options, living, momentous, forced,[1] which that struggle engenders, belief, which is the act of *having liefer*, choosing one possibility out of the innumerable others, elects the direction of safety and o'erleaps uncertainty by action. When it does so with repeated success, it is reason, and the world it so binds satisfies "the sentiment of rationality."

[1] Cf. *The Will to Believe, loc. cit.*

Further, for the reason that reality is a congeries of struggling entities, its ultimate form and character depend more on any single individual or group within that congeries than on the mass as a whole. The salvation of man, consequently, is not preordained, but neither is it foreclosed. That it does not reside, for James, in any external assurance gained through pre-existent "deeper" or higher being, as Bergson thinks, is obvious. Human salvation must inevitably be salvation by humanity. Nor human salvation alone. The gods themselves, if gods there be, may need our help and require perhaps to be sustained even as men sustain one another. Life, for this reason, can be, from the moral point of view, only what each man makes it. Its value lies in the conquest of the evil he, as an individual, finds in it, its literal reformation according to his personal lights. Civilization is such a reformation, such a harmonization of an alien nature with human nature, such a conversion of the foreignness of being into intimacy and ease. Now in civilization, whose history is the history of

mankind, nothing has been so potently direct-
ive as the individual. Himself the field of
persistent choosing, of a battle for existence
between possibilities, he himself is the seat of
what value reality has. This value relates to
his inward demands, his beliefs and desires
and strivings, and its compulsion upon him
is not the compulsion of a pressure from without; it is that of an inward acceptance. There
is no infallible authority, no dominating *élan*.
Obligation exists for the individual on his own
recognition and thereon alone. Consequently
the good of one man is easily the poison of
another, and conversely. The moral universe,
too, is not a monarchy but a federal republic.
Its positive mark is not certainty; its positive mark is hope and fear. If men were
really optimists and pessimists, they would
be unanimous in action. But history is the
history of attempted transmutations of evil
into good, of actions impossible without
belief in the efficacy of change; i.e., without hope and fear. Morally the universe is
melioristic.

Hence, what is of the highest importance in the general improvement cannot, of course, be the generality, and must be the individual. Society's most precious products are its undisciplinables. Its most creative and masterful dynamic forces are its unaccountable geniuses. Their function is that of a ferment, which sets loose and gives direction to the dormant and blind energies stored up in peoples. What were Germany without Bismarck? England without Bob Clive? Athens without Pericles? Once an individual of genius arises, he becomes a point of bifurcation, a cross-roads for society. If, in his nature, spontaneity or inventiveness is stronger than imitation, and if the environment responds to him favorably, the whole of society goes following after him, realizing undreamed-of powers, accomplishing unthought-of masteries. If not, he pays for being different by becoming the object of society's laughter and hatred. And any other view that denies this power to individuality is "an utterly vague and unscientific conception, a lapse from modern scientific determinism into the most ancient oriental fatalism." For fundamentally only the individual must be reckoned, whether conceived deterministically as by "science" or indeterministically as by radical empiricism. "The notion that a people can run itself and its affairs anonymously is now well known to be the silliest of absurdities. Mankind does nothing save through initiative on the part of inventors, great or small, and imitation by the rest of us. These are the sole factors active in social progress."[1] In the winning of the world and the amelioration of reality, the individual counts first, and therefore counts most.

The winning of the world! But what, in the end, is won? There is civilization, but how is civilization better than crude nature? Only in this: that, in the face of an overwhelming pluralism of existences, it confirms man's humanity to man, rather than abolishes it by absorption in a superhuman *élan*. James is no transcendentalist. *He* is a moralist, a humanist.

[1] *Memories and Studies*, p. 318.

The winning, he teaches,[1] is chiefly an assurance, the active sentiment of rationality, the feeling "of the sufficiency of the present moment, of its absoluteness, the absence of all need to explain it, account for it, or justify it." It is the *fluency* of the movement of our proper life, ever enlarging its range and scope, so that more and more of the environing reality gets *unified*, more and more gets clear. Its empirical content is the world, become a familiar place, in which the oncoming future is more and more assured, evil more and more eliminated, so that the congruity of reality with our spontaneous powers makes itself felt continuously: "there is no 'problem of the good.'" The rationalization of the world consists, in a word, of its civilization, and the sentiment of rationality is the feeling of intimacy, the continuous widening "warmth" of appropriation which naturalizes the alien by dominion of law and the rule of good. Behind this conquest, its very *go* and force, is the will to believe —in politics, in art, or in science; the will to

[1] Cf. *ibid.*, "The Sentiment of Rationality."

believe—the "sort of dumb conviction that the truth must be in one direction rather than another"—the "sort of preliminary assurance that a notion can be made to work." Reaching out far beyond evidence, in the bitter struggle for existence, the fittest belief or conception survives, and, surviving, confirms still more deeply in existence the human value that it both assumes and postulates. Faith thus is only a working hypothesis. Its test is our willingness to act upon it—"to act in a cause the prosperous issue of which is not certified to us in advance." Life is no game with loaded dice; its watchword must be *courage,* not peace. Ever the lonely and courageous soul is winning its livelihood at the hazard of its life, ever the army of mankind follows along the way which that soul has opened. The beginning and the end of that way is humanity. Man hath no aim but man, no destiny but mankind. For ever his choice is of himself alone.

It was to realize and to sustain this choice that the shortcomings of experience were repaired by the hypostatization of ideals—ideals being our instruments and programs of life— particularly of the universally human ideals, which the philosophic tradition, and Bergson with it, designates by the eulogium of reality— the ideals of the unity, eternity, goodness and spirituality of the world, and of the freedom and immortality of man. We have seen how careful James has been to indicate, with respect to most of these, just how much is actually discoverable as direct content of experience, just how much is really *ideal*, is but a standard of value by which our nature masters and judges its environment, a method of controlling the environment, *a mode of functioning proper to the creative intelligence of mankind.* In the large, and in the long run, the world is manifold, chaotic, chanceful, evil, a struggle for existence of innumerable entities whose stuff is temporal. These ideals are philosophic desiderates, not actual contents of experience; programs to be realized, not origins nor results to rest in. Objects of belief, they are believed in at constant risk, a risk that involves "courage weighted with responsibility—such courage as the Nelsons and Washingtons never failed to show after they had taken everything into account that might tell against their success and made every provision to minimize disaster." It is the courage of knowledge, not of illusion. If there are risks, "it is better to face them open-eyed than to act as if we did not know them to be there."[1] And to rest at ease in belief as a compensatory substitute for reality, to hypostatize its objects, by no matter what feeling or argument, is to be blind. "Openness of eye" is their watchful use in the reconstruction and discovery of reality.

Even with respect to the most apparently inward and ultimate compensatory ideal, this openness of eye is necessary. If men do in fact survive after death, that fact, like the existence of the gods, must reveal itself as a datum of immediate experience. It must be subjected to the control and the tests which science applies to all data of experience.

[1] *The Will to Believe*, Preface, p. xi.

*P*ersonally James was skeptical of the evidence for survival after death and unconcerned about such survival. To him, as to all great humanists, humanity was a *quality* not a quantity, and it was with the excellences, not the duration of our natures, that he occupied himself. But the belief in "immortality," an expression of our innermost nature, was to his humane view even more entitled to the tests of verification than other beliefs. If we believe, therefore, let there be no obstructions in the way of free investigation. Let belief launch itself into the regions where its object is said to hide. Let it bring the light of honest and just thought and investigation into those, let it enter courageously into the struggle for survival among facts and ideas, ready and glad to die if need be. For if reality is really a fluxful congeries of beings, and everything must ultimately lapse, the important question for man is not "how long" but "how good" is the existence out of which he builds his life. "There is no conclusion," James writes measuredly in the very last

paper his hand touched. "There is no conclusion. What has concluded that we might
conclude in regard to it? There are no
fortunes to be told and there is no advice to
be given—Farewell."[1]

For Bergson, it will be remembered, there
is a conclusion, and that conclusion has been
prefigured from the beginning. The conquest
of death is implied metaphysically, not to be
verified experientially. Man is born at home
in the world, a microcosm essentially at one
with it. For James the difference of man from
the world is the fundamental thing. He is
not born at home in it, he *makes* a home of it.
Metaphysically and morally his life is self-
grounded, and his enmities and friendships
are equally attended with risk. He makes
his destiny as an excellence, a value, not as
a period of time. It resides in character rather
than in length of days, and its watchword
is Courage. By facing the risk open-eyed,
man may master it, and if he fails, he will
win by failing in so far as he has surrendered

[1] *Memories and Studies*, p. 410.

nothing of his nature or his values to the enemy, in so far as he is able to say with Job, "I know that he will slay me; I have no hope: nevertheless will I maintain mine integrity before him."

INDEX

INDEX

Activity, internal, 110, note; creative, 125; James on, 171 f.

Animal, place of, in evolution, 136.

Antinomies, 140 f.

Appearance, evil as, 3; idea as, 88.

Aristotle, theory of knowledge of, 61, 67.

Auscultation, intellectual, 72.

Belief as "sentiment of rationality," 231.

Berkeley, 7.

Bernard, St., 64, 65.

Body, the organic, 211; and personality, 214; and spirit, 221.

Boehme, 64.

Boutroux, É., 47, 48.

Brain, human, in evolution, 137 f.; importance of, 209.

Causation, James on, 174.

Cause and freedom, 123.

Chance, 173 f.

Change, 120 f.; James on, 175.

Compensations in discourse, 6.

Compensatory desiderates, 7, 10, 15, 28.

Concept and percept, 89; Bergson on, 98; James on, 98.

Concepts, 131; status of, 146 f., 167 f.

Consciousness, 179, 210; compounding of, 150; human, 212; and the present, 215.

Continuity, 156, 157.

Control and intuition, 79; as truth, 101.

Courage, 237, 241.

Creative evolution, drama of, 132 f.

Dante, 64.

Descartes, 1.

Desiderates, philosophic, 4.

Determinism, 124.

Duration, 76, 77; hypostatized, 89, note; magnitude of intervals of, 122, 128.

Eckhardt, 64.

Élan vital, relation to Platonic Idea, 108, note; as reality, 113; as the good, 200.

Empiricism, true, 71.

Epicureans, 59.

Experience, James's characterization of, 159; Bergson on religious, 196; as philosophy, 204.

Fallacies of traditional metaphysics, 143.

Flournoy, 47, 49.

245

Index

CPSIA information can be obtained
at www.ICGtesting.com
Printed in the USA
BVOW08s2323110517

483903BV00013B/281/P